what do we know and what should we do about...?

authoritarian regimes

what do we know and what should we do about...?

authoritarian regimes

Natasha Lindstaedt

1 Oliver's Yard
55 City Road
London EC1Y 1SP

2455 Teller Road
Thousand Oaks
California 91320

Unit No 323-333, Third Floor, F-Block
International Trade Tower
Nehru Place, New Delhi – 110 019

8 Marina View Suite 43-053
Asia Square Tower 1
Singapore 018960

Editor: Michael Ainsley
Assistant editor: Sarah Moorhouse
Production editor: Imogen Roome
Copyeditor: Diana Chambers
Proofreader: Brian McDowell
Marketing manager: Fauzia Eastwood
Cover design: Wendy Scott
Typeset by: C&M Digitals (P) Ltd, Chennai, India
Printed in the UK

Library of Congress Control Number: 2023946581

British Library Cataloguing in Publication data

A catalogue record for this book is available from the British Library.

ISBN 978-1-5296-7030-1
ISBN 978-1-5296-7029-5 (pbk)

At Sage we take sustainability seriously. Most of our products are printed in the UK using responsibly sourced papers and boards. When we print overseas we ensure sustainable papers are used as measured by the Paper Chain Project grading system. We undertake an annual audit to monitor our sustainability.

contents

about the series

Every news bulletin carries stories that relate in some way to the social sciences – most obviously politics, economics and sociology, but also, often, anthropology, business studies, security studies, criminology, geography and many others.

Yet, despite the existence of large numbers of academics who research these subjects, relatively little of their work is known to the general public.

There are many reasons for that, but arguably, it is that the kinds of formats that social scientists publish in, and the way in which they write, are simply not accessible to the general public.

The guiding theme of this series is to provide a format and a way of writing that addresses this problem. Each book in the series is concerned with a topic of widespread public interest, and each is written in a way that is readily understandable to the general reader with no particular background knowledge.

The authors are academics with an established reputation and a track record of research in the relevant subject. They provide an overview of the research knowledge about the subject, whether this is long established or reporting of the most recent findings, widely accepted or still controversial. Often in public debate there is a demand for greater clarity about the facts, and that is one of the things the books in this series provide.

However, in social sciences, facts are often disputed and subject to different interpretations. They do not always, or even often, 'speak for themselves'. The authors therefore strive to show the different interpretations or the key controversies about their topics, but without getting bogged down in arcane academic arguments.

Not only can there be disputes about facts, but also there are almost invariably different views on what should follow from these facts. And in any case, public debate requires more of academics than just to report facts; it is also necessary to make suggestions and recommendations about the implications of these facts.

Thus, each volume also contains ideas about 'what we should do' within each topic area. These are based on the authors' knowledge of the field, but also, inevitably, on their own views, values and preferences. Readers may not agree with them, but the intention is to provoke thought and a well-informed debate.

Chris Grey, Series Editor
Professor of Organization Studies
Royal Holloway, University of London

introduction

What are the trends in authoritarianism?

- Rising levels of autocratisation.
- Rising levels of personalism.

Nearly one year after Russia invaded Ukraine on the 24th of February 2022, the war has cost Russia over $80 billion (not including discarding the $11 billion spent investing in the Nord Stream 2), Russia has faced unprecedented economic sanctions and economic turmoil, the Kremlin has become an international pariah, and there have been over 100,000 Russian casualties (Ellyat, 2022; *Kyiv Independent*, 2022; Stewart and Ali, 2022). Nevertheless, contrary to expectations, public opinion polls in 2022 showed that 70 per cent of the Russian public seems to support the 'special operation' in Ukraine (Volkov and Kolesnikov, 2022). How has Vladmir Putin been able to convince his population that a costly war with Ukraine – a country where Russians have an estimated 11 million relatives – is justified (Hopkins, 2022)? Furthermore, how is Putin still so popular? His approval rating in 2023 is at a whopping 82 per cent (Levada Centre, 2023). After all the challenges facing the average Russian today, how on earth is this possible? Wasn't Putin taking a huge gamble that would eventually lead to his being ousted from power?

Although Putin's actions were risky, the answer as to why he was able to take on such risks lies with how modern authoritarian regimes (and autocratising regimes) exercise control over their citizens. When we think of autocracies, this might conjure up images of dictators repressing their citizens and ruling with an iron fist. However, modern dictators rely much more on manipulating information than outright repression (Guriev and Treisman, 2022). At first glance, it may seem that there are fewer regimes capable of the types of repression that characterised the totalitarian regimes of the past. But the toolkit of authoritarian regimes has expanded to now include forms of control that would not have been possible before the improvements made to technology. And in contrast to the Cold War era where totalitarian regimes attempted to brainwash the public to create an undyingly loyal citizenry, autocrats today also use propaganda to generate apathy and sow confusion.

In the case of Russia, Putin has skilfully used his propaganda machine to feed disinterest both in politics and in challenging the regime. Because of this, he is able to take tremendous risks, without facing the level of dissent to his rule that would be necessary to topple him from power. Putin has also managed to control almost all the media in Russia, preemptively stifling any criticism of his rule. Essentially, Putin has been able to convince much of the Russian public that he knows what he's doing. Concurrently, in the past several decades Putin has slowly concentrated more power into his own hands at home (this will be discussed in more detail in a later section of this chapter), while becoming more aggressive in promoting authoritarian values abroad.

The rising level of authoritarianism in Russia is just one example, but examples abound of countries becoming more authoritarian and using a different set of tools to control their populations. Taking advantage of surveillance technology, producing an onslaught of false narratives about the regime and using sham elections to provide an air of legitimacy are some of the commonly used methods that autocrats use to maintain themselves in power.

And it's not just that the methods used by authoritarian regimes have evolved, but *where* authoritarianism is spreading. Because the tools (such as the manipulation of information) used by autocrats are more palatable to non-authoritarian publics, we are seeing a harmonisation of strategies to exercise control across a wide spectrum of regimes, including in some cases, regimes that were once considered to be consolidated democracies.

To understand the threat of authoritarianism, the book offers a background chapter to define what authoritarian regimes are. (Note: we use the terms 'dictatorship', 'autocracy' and 'authoritarian regime' interchangeably.) We explain how regimes are classified and conceptualise what we mean by autocratisation. This chapter is then followed by an explanation of the known components of modern authoritarianism, or how autocrats (and would-be autocrats) stay in power using pseudo-democratic institutions, manipulation of information and technology, and soft and sharp power. The book then looks at what we are still working to better understand – that is, how citizens, protest movements, civil society organisations and NGOs are responding to modern authoritarianism. The book then closes by looking at the new authoritarian threat, summing up the important conclusions, and signposting areas for future research. To get us started, we first look at the patterns and trends of authoritarianism around the globe.

The landscape of authoritarianism: a sea of dictatorships

In spite of the optimism for democracy that characterszed the post-Cold War era, as of 2022, 70 per cent of the world's population lives under autocracy (or about 5.4 billion people), and there are no signs that authoritarianism is going anywhere (Varieties of Democracy, 2022). It may be hard to believe, but most people in the world live in a dictatorship. Even more shocking, the level of democracy is similar to what citizens experienced in 1989; there are fewer liberal democracies, and electoral autocracies are the second most common regime type, the home to 3.4 billion people (ibid.). Electoral democracy, sometimes referred to as 'flawed democracy', is the most common regime type, but this is only because both liberal democracies and electoral autocracies are backsliding – or are becoming less democratic.

Table 1.1 Types of regimes in 2022

Types of regimes in 2022	
Close autocracies	33
Liberal democracies	32
Electoral democracies	58
Electoral autocracies	56

Source: Varieties of Democracy, 2022

What does this mean? Well, there is an increasing number of closed autocracies (for more on that, see Chapter 2), as regimes that once paid some lip service to democracy have gone full-blown authoritarian. As of 2022, there are 33 closed autocracies (as Table 1.1 shows), where 2.2 billion people live. These are regimes that are not even trying to appear to be democratic. After years of competitive authoritarianism (or electoral autocracy), Cambodia, led by Hun Sen since 1985, completely shut down the media, civil society groups and any political opponents to the ruling Cambodian People's Party (CPP). Without any opposition, the CPP was able to win all 125 seats in the National Assembly in 2018 (Morgenbesser, 2019). Further cementing the regime's power, in 2022, mass trials were held for over 100 political opponents (Strangio, 2022). In the following section, we discuss what we mean by autocratisation, or the process of how countries like Cambodia become more autocratic.

An era of autocratisation

As the previous section noted, we are currently experiencing a period of autocratisation, with more countries autocratising (42) than democratising

(14) in 2022.[1] Autocratisation (sometimes also referred to as 'democratic backsliding', 'democratic decay', 'democratic decline' and/or 'democratic erosion'), is the deterioration of institutional checks on government power, such as from the legislature, judiciary, constitution, and independent media (Bermeo, 2016; Maeda, 2010). Autocratisation constitutes the undermining of democratic institutions, governance and transparency, and it takes place through a series of discrete changes in the rules and informal procedures that shape not only elections, but also civil liberties and political rights and accountability. There could also be increasing power of actors that do not have electoral accountability, such as shadow leaders and multinational corporations (Ercan and Gagnon, 2014).

By using the term 'autocratisation', this denotes that the process can take place in a democracy or an autocracy because it constitutes a deliberate process of regime change that is moving towards autocracy regardless of the point of departure. Additionally, it makes the assumption that the level of democracy or autocracy can be observed on a continuum, and thus relies on continuous measures of democracy and autocracy, which will be explained in more detail in Chapter 2.

Some of the most notable cases of autocratisation are taking place in the world's biggest democracies such as in the United States, India and Brazil. These three countries constituted some of the biggest democratic drops, affecting almost two billion people. US democracy was once a model for democracies around the world, but has stumbled with attacks on the rule of law, politicisation of the judiciary, voter suppression laws, dangerous levels of polarisation, a rise in hate crimes, and an attempted insurrection of the Capitol. Politicians have also repeatedly tried to undermine the legitimacy of the mainstream media and questioned the integrity of elections. In India, one of the longest running democracies in Asia, we see a rise in arrests and prosecution of human rights defenders, activists and journalists, while the Muslim community faces increasing harassment (Biswas, 2021). In Brazil, former President Jair Bolsonaro's government captured and/or dismantled

[1] There were 5 coups and 1 self-coup in 2021

some key accountability institutions (e.g., the Attorney General's Office, the Federal Police, environmental and human rights agencies), levelled a sustained attack on the press and the Supreme Court, and cast doubt on the validity of the electoral process. Although Bolsonaro was recently ousted from power in the 2022 presidential election, pro-Bolsonaro rioters (possibly taking a page from Trump's playbook in the US) attacked and vandalised the presidential offices, Brazil's Congress and the Supreme Court on the 8th of January 2023 (Serino, 2023).

While all the above cases have been experiencing a gradual degradation of their democratic systems, they have not experienced democratic breakdowns. With countries that are autocratising, elections may have become less competitive, but they have not been eliminated entirely. Political participation may be restricted and access to resources is narrowed, but the rules supporting universal franchise have not been completely abolished (Tilly, 2003). The media and civil society may be under attack and face intimidation, but they are still free to exist.

In contrast, democratic breakdown is the clear break from democracy, usually exemplified by a coup or the seizure of power of a would-be autocrat or dictator. It is sometimes also referred to as the endpoint of democratic backsliding. This is the point where the method to select a country's leader and/or representatives is no longer based on the will of the people, but through a process that is irregular, unconstitutional and/or fraudulent. For example, in Mali in 2012, a coup was staged that resulted in the ousting of democratically elected leader Amadou Toumani Touré, and the breakdown of Mali's democracy. Touré had been elected twice in 2002 and 2007 in elections that were deemed by the international community as free and fair (Flintoff, 2012). Touré also announced in 2011 that he would abide by the constitution and not try to run for a third term in the upcoming 2012 elections that would take place in July. Before the elections could take place, in March of that year a small group of soldiers attempted a mutiny (aims that are just short of a take-over of the executive) demanding better weapons, ammunition and equipment to battle the insurgent Tuareg community in the North. After chaos ensued, Touré was forced to flee and the military took over (BBC, 2012). Although elections were eventually held again in 2018, Mali has since struggled with conflict and instability, and another coup in 2021, impeded its attempts to return to democracy (Melly, 2021).

The coup that took place in Mali was part of a resurgence of coups, or instances of democratic breakdown. Mali was one of four other countries in 2021 that faced a coup, setting a record in the 21st century for the year with the highest number of coups, up from the average of 1.2 per year (Varieties of Democracy, 2022). In the 1960s, 1970s and 1980s, coups took place much more frequently, with 11 coups taking place in 1963, as Table 1.2 demonstrates. However, there were no successful coups in 2015, and coups seemed to be dying out, while more gradual forms of autocratisation took place. But coups returned with a vengeance in 2021, a sign of the growing brazenness of autocratic actors, and driving the increase in autocratic forms of governance. In addition to Mali, the 2021 coups led to closed autocracies in three other countries – Chad, Guinea and Myanmar.

Table 1.2 Years with the most military coups

1963	11
1966	10
1980	8
1978	7
1965	6
1968	6
1969	6
1975	6

Source: Powell and Thyne, 2022

Autocratic Deepening: It's getting worse

The process of authoritarian regimes becoming increasingly more authoritarian, repressive and arbitrary is a form of autocratisation, known as an 'autocratic deepening' (Pelke and Croissant, 2021). While democratic back-sliding leads to flawed illiberal democracies and hybrid regimes, with autocratic deepening, the starting point is already authoritarian. Autocratic deepening is the most common form of autocratisation, representing two-thirds of autocratisation episodes around the world (Lührmann and Lindberg, 2019).

China has become increasingly authoritarian under Xi Jinping, but while this is a case of autocratisation, it is not *democratic* backsliding. China was never a democracy to start with, and in spite of what the regime may say about itself, there is very little about China that is democratic. Terms that use 'democratic' erosion, decay or decline, for example, can only take place in regimes that are already democratic. Belarus is another example of autocratic deepening because it is already authoritarian but has become even more repressive. You may wonder how it is possible that Belarus could become more autocratic. Well, Belarus managed to accomplish the impossible. During the summer of 2021, Belarus dissolved more than 270 non-profits and public associations, and more than 500 people were arrested for taking part in peaceful protests (Amnesty International, 2022; Louis, 2021). The regime also passed a series of laws in 2021 that targeted political activists and critics of the regime, and made it easier to confiscate private property, revoke their citizenship and implement the death penalty (UNHR, 2023).

Not surprisingly, since the Taliban took over in Afghanistan, the country has become even more authoritarian. Taliban forces have been responsible for targeted killings of civilians, including government officials, journalists and religious leaders. People have been evicted from their homes in retaliation for supporting the former government. Over 70 per cent of Afghan media outlets have been closed, and much more restrictive laws on freedom of the press and speech have been enacted. Protests have also been banned unless they gain the approval of the Ministry of Justice. Women's rights to employment and education have also been curtailed (Human Rights Watch, 2022).

While China, Belarus and Afghanistan are closed autocracies that are somehow finding ways to become more autocratic, most of the cases of authoritarian deepening are taking place in electoral autocracies, or autocracies that hold elections and allow some opposition to exist (more on this in Chapter 2). In these types of regimes, marginalising the opposition is a common strategy. In Uganda, President Yoweri Musevni banned rallies during the 2020–1 campaign season and had his security forces shoot at the supporters of charismatic opposition leader, Robert Kyagulanyi, killing 54 people (Hilsum, 2021; Taylor, 2021). Other leaders and supporters of the opposition were arbitrarily arrested and have faced torture in prison. In Nicaragua, President Daniel Ortega revoked the legal status of the main opposition parties to ensure his victory in the 2021 elections, winning his fourth consecutive term (Kahn and Aburto, 2022).

The case of Nicaragua merits taking a closer look. Several decades ago, Nicaragua held relatively free and fair elections, and at least was trying to be democratic; by 2021, Ortega was cracking down on all of his political opponents (46 were arrested and put on trial in 2022) and he placed his biggest competitor, Christiana Chamorro, under house arrest (BBC, 2021). The trials of those arrested were full of violations to the law, and were considered a total farce (Kahn and Aburto, 2022). And elections weren't the only target for the Ortega regime. In 2022, a law was passed that gave the Nicaraguan government the power to close any NGO that was critical of the regime (Associated Press, 2022). Press freedoms have also deteriorated and crossing the line results in swift punishment. In 2021, one of the largest newspapers, *La Prensa*, had its offices raided, and its publisher was detained and imprisoned for publishing news stories that were critical of the regime. After the regime revoked the licences of 17 media companies in 2022, over 120 journalists fled Nicaragua (Castillo, 2022). Nicaragua has dropped all semblance of democracy and has gone full-blown authoritarian.

In addition to Nicaragua, Turkey, Iran, Yemen, Syria, Venezuela, Bangladesh, El Salvador, Mali, Thailand and Serbia are just some examples of a growing number of autocratic regimes that are deepening.

Personalism: It's All About Me!

Another trend is the rise of personalism. Personalism constitutes the process of power being concentrated in one person's hands, or the political domination of one single leader. With personalism, political allegiance is tied to a person rather than to a political party or ideology. The leader's personality and charisma are more important than rules and institutions, and policies are driven by the leader's whims (Frantz et al., 2021). Essentially, the personalist leader wants to be worshipped by everyone and doesn't want anyone telling them what to do. For some scholars, the hallmarks of personal rule include permanency in office, personalisation of the media, building a cult of personality, deinstitutionalisation, and creating a patronage system (Baturo and Elkink, 2021). Not all personalist rulers exhibit these characteristics, but personalist leaders demonstrate most of these criteria.

Unfortunately, authoritarian regimes have become more personalistic than they were in the past. During the Cold War, personalist regimes accounted for only 23 per cent of all dictatorships. Roughly three decades later, the number of personalist regimes has almost doubled, with personalist forms of authoritarian rule constituting 40 per cent of all dictatorships (Kendall-Taylor et al., 2017). Personalist regimes aren't necessarily more authoritarian, but personalist rule elongates the tenure that one leader is in power, and this comes at the expense of development and national security. This leads to more policy instability and more erratic conflict behaviour (Frantz and Ezrow, 2011). As personalist leaders tend to be surrounded by sycophants instead of experts, they lack solid advice in their decision-making, and the lack of checks on their power means they are free to take on risky decisions without accountability. They also like to promote inexperienced family members to important positions in the government and military. With zero experience, former dictator Rafael Trujillo of the Dominican Republic promoted his son Ramfis to the rank of brigadier general. He was only 9 years old at the time. Ignoring the old adage that you shouldn't mix business with pleasure, Ortega in Nicaragua saw no issue with having his wife Rosario Murillo as his Vice President in 2017. The other issue is that when personalist regimes are ousted, they are more often than not replaced by other forms of personalist authoritarian rule, if not state failure (Ezrow and Frantz, 2013).

China and Russia are two notable cases of regimes that are becoming increasingly personalistic. China has been run by the Communist

Party (CCP) since 1949, but during the Mao Zedong years there were high levels of personalism. Since Mao's death in 1976, the regime and Communist Party became better institutionalised or more rule-bound. Some key innovations were fixed terms of office, term limits, a mandatory retirement age, and regular meetings of CCP institutions, such as of the Central Committee and the Politburo (Chen et al., 2005). But politics has become increasingly personalised under Xi Jinping, who took over in 2013 (Ruwitch, 2023). Xi first broke precedent by not promoting a successor at the 19th Party Congress in October 2017 (Shirk, 2018). Then the two-term limit was abolished for the president at the National People's Congress in 2018. Besides these notable changes, Xi is also in charge of almost everything. Key agencies and commissions are chaired by him exclusively, or must report to him directly. A group that Xi chairs on deepening reforms has become a powerful shadow State Council. Xi has also surrounded himself by loyalists. In March 2023, Li Qiang was appointed to Premier, the second most powerful position in the Politburo Standing Committee. The role of premier used to have more autonomy, and Li's predecessor Li Keqiang was seen as a threat to Xi. Li Qiang, however, has a decades-long relationship with Xi, and is willing to execute Xi's decisions with no questions asked (Yu, 2022). Two other close Xi devotees, Han Zheng and Zhao Leji, were awarded the roles of vice president and head of parliament, respectively (Ruwitch, 2023). Xi also has complete hold on the People's Liberation Army (PLA), and scholars have noted that no other Chinese Communist Party leader, outside of Mao, had exercised this much control (Fewsmith and Nathan, 2019; Gueorguiev, 2018; Shirk, 2018).

Xi has also cultivated a personality cult, going by the nickname of Xi Dada, or Father Xi, and has leveraged the mass media to constantly promote his image, and even the image of his wife, famous opera singer Peng Liyuan (Luqiu, 2016). Videos have showcased their love story, and one video has a montage of Xi holding hands with Peng while she belts out soaring patriotic songs in praise of the Communist Party (Fan et al., 2016). Xi's portrait is also ubiquitous, and his photo is also suspiciously much bigger than other Politburo members, a clear departure from the post-Mao era (Yin and Flew, 2018). State officials constantly fawn over him, while the curriculum has been updated to promote his calm demeanour and persona as a man of the people (Hart, 2021). The messages being conveyed are clear: China cannot survive without Xi.

The rise in personalism is even more severe in Russia. Constant changes have been made to the constitution through federal laws, presidential decrees and decisions of the constitutional courts which have increased the president's powers (Burkhardt, 2020). This contrasts with the power balance while Yeltsin was in power. During Yeltsin's presidency, there were many parties and politicians in the legislature that opposed him. Under Putin, there's an absence of any actor or organ that could challenge Putin's power. This took place through a series of notable actions. By 2006 or so, Putin had centralised power into the Presidential Administration (Fish, 2017).[2] The upper chamber of the legislature is now appointed and has virtually no power. The heads of the legislature are also de facto Putin nominees, and the legislature never passes any legislation that would ever go against Putin's wishes (Fish, 2018). Putin also established full control over the Central Electoral Commission to ensure that electoral contests always go his way.

Because power is so personalised under Putin, there are some key differences with today's Russia and the Soviet Union. In contrast to the Soviet period, the incumbent party is poorly institutionalised, without a clear political ideology. Although almost all politicians have joined his United Russia Party, if Putin were to leave power, the party would collapse with him, while the Communist Party survived the deaths and resignations of ten different leaders (Bunce, 2017). The United Russia party was founded solely to support Putin, and for the most part, Putin sees it as a necessary nuisance. The party exists as a 'parking lot' for Russian politicians who crave power and money.

The Russian president also has the power to appoint the judiciary unchallenged, and judges make no important decisions. In terms of the

[2]This is the only comparable organ to the Communist Party under Stalin

law, Putin retains ultimate power – he can enact, alter and ignore the laws at his own will (Fish, 2017). Putin also established control over the security institutions by hand-picking the top police officials and military elites.

Putin also exercises much more control over the regional governments. In Russia, new laws were adopted in 2000 that stripped governors of their automatic membership to the upper chamber, the Federation Council. Putin then ensured that regional governments were much more reliant on Moscow for funding and there was more oversight of their activities. A federal inspector was sent to each province to report back on the governors. Additionally, seven new federal administrative districts were created, called super regions, that report back to Putin, and twenty new federal agencies were created to oversee tasks such as regulating the media, tax collection, pension funds, and property rights, that reported to Moscow, which enabled him to exercise better control. After a terrorist attack on Russia in September 2004 (which Putin blamed on regional governments being too weak), Putin scrapped the rules so that governors were no longer elected but were nominated by regional legislatures, which he himself appointed (Fish, 2018).

In Russia, there is little question about who is in charge. Nevertheless, in contrast to Xi, Stalin or other personalist leaders, Putin has not decided to build a personality cult. There are few statues of Putin in Russia, and Putin's portrait is not plastered everywhere. Nevertheless, Russian state television launched a weekly television show called *Moscow. Kremlin. Putin.*, which focuses on Putin's achievements (Baturo and Elkink, 2021). The state-run media has also carefully crafted Putin's image of an athletic sportsman, with an ultra-macho persona, proficient at horseback riding, judo, fishing and ice hockey, to name but a few. As with any personalist leader, it is difficult to discern the degree to which the public actually buys into it. Based on surveys, it appears to be working, with Putin recording some of the highest approval ratings while in power (Cook, 2023).

And Putin is not the only one. The 21st century has been a good time to be a dictator.

Conclusion

After decades of democracy promotion and assistance, democratic values and institutions are being seriously challenged. Most of the world's population now lives in autocracies, and there is a growing number of authoritarian regimes that are completely repressive. Authoritarian powers have also become more aggressive and brazen on the world stage, with the aforementioned Russian invasion of Ukraine a terrifying example of this new phase of authoritarianism. In the face of the disastrous war in Ukraine, Putin and Xi are building a close friendship and a no-limits partnership. All these events are part of the global trends of autocratisation and rising personalism. Nevertheless, while Xi and Putin's regimes appear to be harmonising, these regimes are not the same. In the following chapter, we define dictatorship in more detail, and explain the different types of dictatorship and degrees of authoritarianism. We also look at how dictatorship today differs from dictatorships in the past, and in what ways it is more of the same.

background

- How do we measure and classify regimes?

As the Introduction demonstrated, we have more electoral autocracies and more closed autocracies than we had nearly a decade ago. To help understand these trends, this chapter will provide an explainer – we'll define and classify authoritarian regimes and the ways in which regimes are becoming more resilient. After first defining what an authoritarian regime is, we lay out how past classifications of non-democracies differ from how we understand authoritarianism today. We then explain the two types of measures of authoritarian regimes – those that measure authoritarian regimes on a continuum and those that use categorical measurements. Throughout the chapter, we offer examples of these classifications and highlight the patterns that have emerged from these areas of research.

Defining Autocracy

Although there are many ways of defining autocracy, authoritarian regimes constitute any regime that does not have turnover in power of the executive

(Geddes, 1999, 2005). Regimes that have meaningful elections are democracies, while those that don't are autocracies. Additionally, authoritarian regimes don't uphold civil liberties and fail to implement the rule of law. There are also usually few mechanisms to hold those who abuse power accountable, and elites are often free to use the state for their own private gain without facing repercussions. Constitutions may exist on paper only, or are written in ways to constrain the press, civil society and the wider public.

At the heart of understanding dictatorships is the idea that they care first and foremost about their own political survival. True, all political actors also care about this as well, but in democracies mechanisms are in place to prevent individuals from being in power forever, from stealing from the state, and for ensuring that information flows freely and decisions are made more collectively with citizen input. These vertical (from elections), horizontal (from courts and legislatures), discursive (from the media) and diagonal forms (from civil society) of accountability help to protect citizens. Dictatorships don't have the same type of safeguards, which can result in very different outcomes.

Thus, one of the inherent weaknesses of authoritarian regimes is that a dictator's quest for survival can lead to perverse outcomes for the public. Where the number of decision-makers narrows, this makes it even more unlikely that the policies will be implemented that benefit the public good. The dictator may be worried that technocrats will threaten his personal power and purposely purge experts. Dictatorships may worry that transparency about an issue will affect the regime's legitimacy and cause unrest, leading to the spread of false information. A dictator may also be worried that they will soon be ousted from power, leading to the hoarding of the state's coffers. Essentially, the endless pursuit of staying in power has often had dire consequences. As the next section explains, past methods used by dictatorships to hold on to power required unsustainable levels of effort from the state.

Totalitarian or not

In the past, non-democratic regimes were either lumped into one large category, or delineated by whether or not they were totalitarian or authoritarian. In the late 1930s and 1940s, scholars observed a new political phenomenon, the rise of a form of dictatorship that was so all-encompassing that it deserved its own category, which was labelled totalitarianism. The rise of leaders such as Joseph Stalin in the Soviet Union, Adolf Hitler in Germany, and Benito Mussolini in Italy attracted the attention of researchers such as Hannah Arendt (1958: 323–4) who noted that totalitarian regimes demanded 'total, unrestricted, unconditional, and unalterable loyalty of the individual member . . . '[1] Totalitarian regimes were characterised by high levels of power concentrated in the leaders' hands, a personality cult around a highly charismatic leader, the role of a mass party and other organisations of mobilisation, and a massive security organisation with the capabilities to surveil the entire population. Autocracies may possess one or a few of these elements, but possessing all of these elements simultaneously was characteristic of totalitarian regimes.

For Juan Linz (2000), totalitarian regimes were also distinct from authoritarian regimes for not only their level of control over the population, but also for the prominent role of ideology and indoctrinating this ideology in the wider citizenry. Carl Friedrich and Zbigniew Brzezinski identified a 'totalist ideology' as an important characteristic of totalitarian government (1956). The ideology was elaborate, attempting to offer meaning and a deep sense of historical purpose to the regime, and to legitimise the leader in the eyes of the public. Another distinct feature were the efforts that totalitarian regimes placed in mobilising the public, politicising them to be loyal foot soldiers for the regime, and transforming human nature. Every citizen was expected to be fully activated and participating in the state and society (Linz, 2000). Totalitarian regimes are also highly repressive and brutal. Pol Pot's Khmer Rouge regime (1975–9) was responsible for the killing of over a third of the country's 8 million people. In the USSR, forced collectivisation and purges killed 5 million and 1 million people, respectively (Snyder, 2010). Many people also died at the hands of authoritarian leaders, but not on the same scale.

[1] For some scholars Hitler's Germany and Mussolini's Italy were more accurately categorized as fascist and not totalitarian (Alexander, 2004; Kallis, 2002; Morgan, 2003).

Authoritarian regimes, in contrast, have neither the capacity nor the will to surveil, indoctrinate and mobilise their population. Ideology is less important to authoritarian regimes, which prefer to foster political apathy, rather than indoctrinate the regime's world view. Although different forms of repression are used, it was never on the scale seen in totalitarian regimes. There was also no human army of citizen informants spying on one another, or a massive secret police in authoritarian regimes. Political parties exist in authoritarian regimes, but they are mostly focused on stealing elections rather than on marshalling citizens to be loyal foot soldiers. Authoritarian leaders sometimes build a personality cult around their charismatic persona, but not always. Citizens also have a little more freedom to live their lives, without being intruded upon by the state at every turn.

The same could not be said of North Korea, one of the few states that still meets the threshold of being totalitarian today. North Korea's government, under the Kim dynasty (1948–), has sought to activate its citizens to be fully committed to the regime. North Koreans are indoctrinated with the juche ideology of self-reliance, which provides guidelines in every field of human endeavour (Oh and Hassing, 2000). What this means is that North Koreans are inculcated from an early age to believe that the Supreme Leader is a messianic type of figure, an eternal president who possesses superhuman powers (Byman and Lind, 2010; Kim, 2001). The regime also has total control over the media, and citizens are unable to access any alternative information, other than the propaganda that they are forced to consume by the regime.

In addition to the relentless propaganda, North Korea is also characterised by a climate of terror that is generated by the pervasive secret police and citizen informants. No one is exempt from investigation and from being watched, and anyone suspected of being disloyal faces a severe punishment (Oh and Hassig, 2000). Those who commit minor offences may be forced to go to a re-education camp, while those accused of more serious transgressions are sent to political prison camps. A 2004 survey of refugees who had escaped to China after a stint in a prison camp confirmed that the practices in these camps were inhumane, with 90 per cent reportedly witnessing forced starvation, 60 per cent witnessing deaths by torture and 27 per cent witnessing executions (Haggard and Nolan, 2009). To further instil fear in its population, it is not just the accused who face punishments, but his or her entire family (Byman and Lind, 2010). Although North Korea is one of the poorest and most oppressive countries in the world, there appear to be no signs of regime collapse.

Different ways of categorising dictatorships today

In the study of dictatorships, the distinction between totalitarian and authoritarian regimes was a useful starting point, helping us to better understand not only different degrees of dictatorship, but also different types of dictatorship. Nevertheless, the study of dictatorships went through some major shifts. Most totalitarian regimes collapsed or evolved into autocracies, as totalitarianism was difficult to maintain, with the exception of North Korea. Additionally, it was not just totalitarian regimes that were collapsing, but authoritarian regimes as well. The Third (1970s and 1980s) and Fourth (1990s) Waves of democratisation led to the ousting of many old dictatorships. Although authoritarian breakdown took place and new leaders were elected, the regimes were failing to fully democratise. It initially looked as though there was no longer a clear line between democracy and autocracy, with many regimes transitioning to democracy. Scholars eventually reconsidered that many of these transitional regimes were not on a pathway to democracy. Instead, these regimes were examples of new forms of authoritarianism. These regimes are sometimes referred to as 'competitive authoritarian regimes', 'liberalised autocracies' and 'electoral authoritarian regimes'.

As Chapter 3 will explain in greater detail, these new forms of authoritarianism use formally democratic institutions that mask 'the reality of authoritarian domination' (Diamond, 2002: 24). New forms of authoritarianism have electoral institutions that perpetuate regime survival instead of turnover in power. Simply put, these new types of authoritarian regimes are not in the process of transitioning to democracy; they are actually fairly resilient in their position.

Although these new forms of authoritarianism were resilient, they were more competitive and less repressive than other dictatorships. Continuous typologies of dictatorship emphasise the various gradients of dictatorship, which also allows for more comprehensive definitions of autocracy. For the most part, continuous measures of authoritarianism assess how undemocratic regimes are, and not the other way around (although there are exceptions). In other words, autocracies are measured by how much freedom they provide, such as in the areas of speech, religion, press and association; how fair and free their elections are; how consistently and robustly the rule of law is applied; how strong the checks are on the executive from the legislative branch and the judiciary; how well institutionalised the bureaucracy is (by this we mean that the bureaucracy follows rules and procedures rather than accepts that bribes and positions are filled by those with expertise) and how well it is able to function and implement policies. As the introduction highlighted, those regimes that fall somewhere in the middle of this spectrum are often referred to as 'grey zone regimes' or 'hybrid regimes' (see Diamond, 1999; Collier and Levitsky, 1997; Carothers, 2002; Hadenius and Teorrel, 2006). At the end of the spectrum are closed autocracies. But what do we mean by closed autocracies?

Closed autocracies are regimes that have no democratic mechanisms for turnover in power. Either the elections are a foregone conclusion and are plagued by massive fraud or there are no elections at all. The leader inherits his or her position, or was designated as the next leader by the incumbent. The legislature is filled with party members who were either appointed by the dictator or were beneficiaries of unfair competition. The judiciary exists, but it follows the direction of the executive. Closed autocracies also have few outlets for free expression. Those who speak out against the regime face retribution; the press is muzzled by restrictive laws or engages in self-censorship; there are rules that prohibit protesting or independent organisation. Afghanistan, China, Chad, Syria, Turkmenistan, Saudi Arabia, Yemen, Myanmar, Cuba, Bahrain, South Sudan, Uzbekistan, Laos, Iran, Qatar and Guinea, are examples of closed autocracies.

In contrast to authoritarian regimes of the past that tolerated almost no opposition, new forms of authoritarianism (heretofore referred to as electoral authoritarian regimes) allowed the opposition to run in elections. These elections were also free of massive fraud, as the results were not entirely predetermined, and the incumbent may win by smaller margins. However, in contrast to democracies, the elections never lead to turnover in power and the outcome is pretty much guaranteed. Why is this the case? Because the playing field is not fair at all, and incumbents have access to a variety of state resources that can help them ensure victory.

The legislature is another point of distinction between closed and electoral authoritarian regimes. In closed authoritarian regimes, the legislature holds absolutely no power, and the same can be said for the judiciary. In contrast, the judiciary and the legislature in electoral authoritarian regimes occasionally challenge the executive, and the opposition can use the legislature to meet and organise. Although this is mostly just a safety valve to deal with discontent, the opposition has a little more leeway to manoeuvre in electoral authoritarian regimes (Levitsky and Way, 2002).

There are also a few avenues for expression in electoral authoritarian regimes. Although these liberties are fairly limited, there are ways in which citizens can occasionally express themselves. The media is also not completely state owned or controlled, and the media is able to occasionally offer criticisms of the regime, although at its own risk. In Venezuela, the media was able to criticise former president Hugo Chávez, but it was also regularly harassed, intimidated and subject to fines and censorship, or was unable to renew its licence. Tough laws were passed that increased penalties for speech that was deemed offensive to the government. As Chávez consolidated more executive power, there was also an increase in the number of television channels and radio stations that were owned by the government.

Gaining control over information is important because new forms of authoritarianism seem to have some interest in generating genuine support from the public. In Singapore, most of its citizens are content with the regime, and view the government as capable in overseeing economic growth, stability, security and prosperity. Ensuring high levels of support makes countries like Singapore easier to govern. For that reason, leaders in many electoral autocracies may care what the public thinks to some extent, and elections may be used to gauge public opinion.

Citizens may be willing to vote for the incumbent regime even without being coerced into doing so, either because they believe the regime is better than the alternative or because they believe there are tangible benefits to supporting the status quo. For this reason, some electoral regimes can sustain themselves for a long time without having to engage in massive fraud. Returning to the Singapore example, the government could hold totally free and fair elections, and the ruling People's Action Party (PAP) would win by a wide margin, without having to use underhand tactics.

From time to time, however, just by holding elections, an electoral autocracy eventually transitions into a democracy. This contrasts with closed autocracies where the opposition is completely shut out and has no chance.[2] In contrast, in electoral autocracies, sometimes elections lead to a win for the opposition (Howard and Roessler, 2006). The case of Mexico illustrates this. Mexico under the ruling Institutional Revolutionary Party (PRI) regime was an electoral autocracy for over eight decades. Elections were mostly free of fraud, but there was only one winner as the PRI was able to take advantage of its control over the media and used state coffers to dole out gifts and other forms of patronage to its supporters. As a result, the PRI was incredibly effective in mobilising voters to the polls. Nevertheless, in the presidential elections in 2000, there was finally a victory for the opposition, the National Action Party (PAN). Although the current state of democracy in Mexico is highly flawed, electoral outcomes are no longer predetermined.

And though Mexico is no longer an electoral authoritarian regime, there are many past and current examples. Other notable examples from

[2] There are few instances of a closed authoritarian regime suddenly holding a free and fair election that leads to turnover in power, without being preceded by significant protest, a revolution, elite removal or external intervention. This is much more likely to happen in an electoral autocracy.

the past include Peru under Alberto Fujimori and Ukraine under Leonid Kuchma. Contemporary examples are Venezuela under Nicolás Maduro, Mozambique under the FRELIMO Party and Nicaragua under Daniel Ortega. Other electoral autocracies include Albania, Angola, Belarus, Cameroon, Hungary, Guatemala, Kazakhstan, Mozambique, Singapore, Tanzania and Turkey – to name a few (Varieties of Democracy, 2022). Elections are held in all of these examples, but there is little doubt who will win. Yet, there is some room for the opposition to exist, and criticisms of the governments have taken place – albeit not without facing some sort of retribution, and there is a bit more power in other institutions. These new forms of authoritarianism differ from the past varieties which had repressive and coercive institutions, and made no attempts to appear democratic.

Some electoral authoritarian regimes attempt to appear more democratic than others, and there is a big variance in the level of democracy within electoral autocracies, and in which ways they are more authoritarian than others. According to the Varieties of Democracy Dataset, the Philippines was recently downgraded to an electoral authoritarian regime, which would put it in the same category as Venezuela and Russia (Varieties of Democracy, 2023). Elections have become more fraught with irregularities in the Philippines, but there is more uncertainty about the outcome relative to Russia and Venezuela. Although Manila has become increasingly hostile towards the media (it has been noted as one of the most dangerous places in the world for journalists), academics and activists, there is a much greater degree of freedom to protest and participate for the average citizen in the Philippines compared to Venezuela or Russia. That being said, the rule of law in the Philippines is rapidly deteriorating and extrajudicial killings of activists, journalists and drug dealers/users have become commonplace. In spite of this, there is a great deal of variance in terms of the levels of authoritarianism between the Philippines on one hand, and Russia and Venezuela on the other, which are equally repressive. This begs the question – is there a way to distinguish between dictatorships that are equally repressive?

While some scholars may argue that authoritarianism is best understood as a matter of degrees from a democratic ideal, others claim that we lose out on understanding some of the nuances between dictatorships, which may be equally autocratic (Frantz and Ezrow, 2011; Geddes, 2005). Barbara Geddes (1999, 2005) and her colleagues (2014) pioneered an approach to disaggregate autocracy based on who holds power: who makes decisions, who controls access to patronage, and which segments of society support the regime, known as a categorical classification of dictatorship. Based on these criteria, Geddes argues that autocracies can be designated as personalist, single party or military regimes, or some combination of these. Monarchies, where a regime is led by a ruling family, are an additional category. By categorising regimes based on who holds power, this offers important insights for a host of different outcomes such as the longevity of the leader, the longevity of the regime, the propensity to go to war, economic stability, the level of repression and the probability of democratising.

It is important to note that there may be personalist regimes that are closed autocracies (such as Belarus under Alexander Lukashenko) and personalist regimes that are electoral autocracies (such as Turkey under Recep Erdoğan). There are also closed autocracies that are single party (such as China under the Communist Party) and electoral autocracies that are single party (such as Mozambique). The same can be said for military regimes. Most monarchies are closed autocracies as they don't hold meaningful elections, but there are some monarchies that allow for more competition than others, such as Kuwait, Jordan and Morocco (which have parliaments), and Saudi Arabia and Bahrain which are much more repressive. We lay out the characteristics of these types of dictatorships below.

Personalist dictatorships see power highly concentrated in the leader's hands, and the leader is unencumbered by rules, institutions or an ideology. The dictator comes to personify the state, and the lines between the state and the leader are blurred (Chehabi and Linz, 1998). The dictator is supported by a small group of elites which narrows in size over time. This elite support group is rarely comprised of experts or technocrats, with the dictator preferring to surround themselves with loyal sycophants or family members that pose little threat to the leader's survival. A political party may exist, but its policy platform mirrors the dictator's interests. Legislative and judicial institutions may also exist, but they function as rubber stamps to the dictator's main agenda. The bureaucracy is hollowed out and stuffed with loyalists who lack expertise and competence.

With virtually no institutional checks on the leader and few voices of reason, personalist dictators make all the important decisions themselves, mostly without much consultation. As a result, they are free to pursue policies that often reflect their personal whims and wild impulses. Muammar Qaddafi, who ruled Libya between 1969 and 2011, replaced the Gregorian calendar with a solar calendar, changing all the months with names that he invented himself. He also forced every Libyan to own chickens to promote self-sufficiency (Black, 2000). While those ideas may sound wacky, it gets weirder. Hastings Banda, who was prime minister and later president of Malawi from 1964 to 1994, decreed that women were forbidden from wearing trousers. Saparmurat Niyazov, who ruled Turkmenistan between 1985 and 2006, banned ballet because he found it dull and forbade newsreaders from wearing make-up (Reuters, 2008). He also had the national flag approved on his own birthday and referred to himself as Turkmenbashi, the father of all Turkmens (Baturo and Elkink, 2021). Personalist leaders are unfettered by the same types of institutions and rules that often constrain other dictatorships, and, as they are constantly told what they want to hear, this can result in one bad idea after another.

True, no dictator rules alone, and even a personalist dictator must balance different competing group interests. However, the elites in personal dictatorships typically owe their positions to personal connections with the leader and not through rising up the ranks in the military or the civil service. Personalist dictators handpick government officials themselves, who are loyal either out of fear of reprisal or due to material rewards. Patronage is incredibly important in personalist dictatorships to maintain the leader in power, but the main beneficiaries are usually just the dictator's small elite support group. This style of governance tends to infect the entire state. Relationships of loyalty and dependence are pervasive; officials occupy office not to perform public service, but to acquire personal wealth vis-à-vis other citizens (Bratton and van de Walle, 1994). In Putin's Russia, state employees act like bandits (Bunce, 2017). Because the state and institutions have become completely dysfunctional, this environment is totally inhospitable for democracy after the personalist regime falls from power.

Unfortunately, since the Cold War ended, personalist dictatorships are on the rise, and 40 per cent of all autocracies are ruled by strongmen (Kendall-Taylor et al., 2017). Examples of personalist dictatorships in power today include Russia (where Vladimir Putin has ruled since 1999), Belarus (where Alexander Lukashenko has ruled since 1994), Rwanda (where Paul Kagame has been in power since 2000), and more recently, Turkey (where Recep Tayyip Erdoğan has been in power since 2003). And although not all of the regimes in the world are personalising, as the previous chapter explained, personalism is on the rise, even in single-party regimes like China.

Single-party dictatorships are regimes in which a single party holds power and controls policy and decision making (Geddes, 1999). The legislature exists, but is mostly filled with party members or supporters of the incumbent party. The judiciary and the state are also loyal to the incumbent party. Some single-party regimes ban other parties altogether, while other single-party regimes allow other political parties to exist and compete in elections. However, these opposition parties have little influence on policy outcomes and have no chance of taking office, as the playing field is so unfair that the incumbent is assured a victory, as in Malaysia until 2018 and Mexico until 2000 (Magaloni and Kricheli, 2010). Examples of single-party dictatorships in power today include China, Laos, Vietnam, Angola and Cuba.

Single-party regimes are distinct from other forms of dictatorship because the party is especially well institutionalised and autonomous from any one leader. Most single party regimes have agreed upon rules for succession, such as term limits for the leader (Geddes, 1999). In Mexico, turnover in the power of the president took place through an election, a process that was known as the 'sexenio'. Returning to the case of China, up until Xi Jinping unravelled the succession rules in place in 2022, Chinese leaders only held power for 10 years, after which power was peacefully transferred to a new leader. When rules for succession are in place, it is less likely that a destabilising power struggle will arise, which enhances the longevity of the regime (Smith, 2005).

The leader in single-party regimes is also not able to make decisions at will. Serious discussions and consultations take place, which slows down the process of decision making and usually results in policy outputs that are consistent and predictable. Parties also tend to be well institutionalised enough to be able to distribute rents to a wide range of citizens, not just elites. As a result of all these factors, single-party regimes tend to experience the fewest coups, enjoy higher economic growth and last the longest compared to other forms of dictatorships, particularly military regimes that last on average for only a few years (Geddes et al., 2014).

Military regimes are regimes where a military junta, or a small group of members of the military, hold power. Thus, members of the executive branch are members of the military who have taken power after a coup. They not only control the security forces, but also control policy making. Although this is a more collegial form of autocracy compared to personalist regimes and there is a degree of consultation involved, there are still fewer decision makers with policy expertise, and the number of individuals involved in consultation is usually much smaller than single-party regimes.

Military rule is not a regime that is led by a man who is in uniform or who at one point may have been in the military. Personalist dictators Idi Amin of Uganda and Rafael Trujillo of the Dominican Republic were military officers, but the military did not rule as an institution because each leader had concentrated so much power in his own hands and had no need to bargain with other officers (Geddes et al., 2014).[3] Personalist dictators manipulate and divide, and conquer factions within the military and gradually marginalise officers from decision making (Geddes et al., 2014). In contrast, in military regimes, the leader has to bargain with the military to govern.

As mentioned, military regimes are notable for not holding on to power for very long. Soldiers may naturally prefer to return to the barracks, and may fear that politicising the military would threaten the organisation's corporate unity. The military cares about its legitimacy and worries about potential splits to the organisation. For this reason, it may stage a coup

[3] Geddes classifies both Trujillo and Amin as personalist dictators

and hold power for a few years, and willingly choose to negotiate their own exit. In contrast to personalist dictators who are likely to cling to power until the bitter end, military regimes see a life after politics, and prefer to leave power officially and on their terms, as long as they can ensure that their corporate interests are met.

Although Myanmar, Thailand and Algeria are a handful of examples where the military is still in power (either directly or behind the scenes), military regimes were much more common in the past. During the 1960s, 1970s and 1980s, military regimes made up about a fifth of the world's autocracies. Military regimes were especially prevalent in Latin America, but also existed in a number of places elsewhere, such as Turkey (1980–3) and Nigeria (1966–79 and 1983–93). Today, the military as an institution still holds tremendous power in countries that experienced military rule. In Brazil, the military remains one of the most powerful lobbies in the country, ensuring that military spending increased even after it stepped down from power and Brazil democratised (Zaverucha and da Cunha Rezende, 2009).

While some military regimes eventually do democratise, the same cannot be said for monarchies. Monarchies are autocracies where a ruling family or a person of royal descent inherits the position of head of state according to practice or the constitution (Hadenius and Teorrell, 2007). The monarchy is not just a ceremonial position, but the ruling family occupies key positions of power, has control over the military and security services, and dictates domestic and foreign policy. Almost all of today's monarchic dictatorships exist in North Africa and the Middle East, with the exception of Brunei (1959–) and Swaziland (1968–).

Monarchies have proved to be extremely resilient. Although the revolutions of the Arab Spring toppled regimes in Yemen, Libya, Tunisia and Egypt, and led to a brutal conflict in Syria, the monarchies of Morocco, Jordan, Saudi Arabia, Oman, Bahrain, Qatar, Kuwait and the United Arab Emirates all remained relatively stable. There are several reasons for this. Monarchies have historical–religious claims to legitimacy and can stand above the fray of different conflicts in society (Yom and Gause, 2012).

Monarchies foster cross-cutting coalitions within society, and have historical alliances with different social constituencies (ibid.). The ruling family also has strong ties to society and the ability to mobilise a diverse network of support. There are also mechanisms in place to distribute patronage to many of their citizens.

Additionally, monarchies often have institutionalised rules of succession, which makes the process of transitioning power more stable. This is not always the case, as there have been instances where monarchic regimes have become embroiled in a power struggle, such as in January 2006, when Sheik Saad was Kuwait's ruler for nine days before being removed by parliament due to his poor health. However, Kuwait's 1962 constitution and 1964 law of succession provided guidelines for deposing an emir in the case of physical or mental incapacity, or an inability to assume responsibilities, and Kuwait was able to weather the political storm.

Conclusion

As this chapter has explained, the major distinguishing feature of a dictatorship is that there is no turnover in power of the executive, which could be run by a host of different actors. Some dictatorships have a military junta in charge, such as in Thailand; some dictatorships are run by a single party, such as Vietnam under the Communist Party; some dictatorships have a ruling family holding power, such as the House of Bolkiah in Brunei; and some dictatorships are led by a strongman, such as Nicolas Maduro in Venezuela. Dictatorships vary by who holds power and by how many individuals are involved in decision making. Dictatorships also vary by how much freedom they offer their citizens, how competitive the mechanisms for turnover in power are, and the strength of institutional checks on the executive. As the chapter explained, while some of these newer forms of authoritarian rule appear to be less repressive and more competitive, this does not mean that they are any less resilient. Not only is authoritarianism on the rise, but authoritarian regimes are lasting longer.

One of the reasons why autocracies have become more durable is that they have made some clever adaptations, although it is not entirely clear the extent to which these adaptations represent a break from the past. On one hand, it could be argued that it is unlikely that totalitarian forms of government that exercise complete control over individuals and information will emerge in the years to come. However, improvements in technology have meant that authoritarian regimes are now much more capable of engaging in some of the same types of behaviour of totalitarian regimes, shaping hearts and minds, but using bots instead of textbooks; spying on their citizens but using facial-recognition technologies instead of undercover agents; blocking information that citizens can access, but instead of banning books certain websites are selectively blocked. Authoritarian regimes have evolved and learned to take up the 'best' practices from both totalitarian regimes and democracies to become more resilient than ever.

In the following chapter, we explain what we *should* know about authoritarian regimes today – namely, how authoritarian regimes have been repackaged. While some aspects of authoritarian rule have significantly changed, the chapter explains to what extent these changes represent 'old wine in new bottles' (De Kadt, 2002).

what do we know about authoritarian regimes?

- Changes in repression (speed bumps).
- Pseudo-democratic institutions.
- Spin dictators (domestic propaganda, flooding).
- A new age of digital authoritarianism (surveillance and censorship).

Are modern authoritarian regimes less autocratic today than in the past? On the surface, autocracies may look more democratic, but a closer look reveals that they have simply been repackaged and are actually more durable than ever. Data from 1946 to1989 showed that the average authoritarian regime only lasted 12 years. In comparison, since the Cold War ended, the average autocracy has lasted more than twenty years (Kendall-Taylor and Frantz, 2014).

So how is it that authoritarian regimes look more democratic, but are lasting longer than ever? Authoritarian regimes actually use institutions of democracy, such as elections, legislatures and judiciaries not only to veil their authoritarian nature, but also to ensure their own survival. These institutions help dictatorships deal more effectively with the opposition, without having to always use force. This does not mean that new authoritarians are totally non-violent. They still use brutal force to target journalists and activists; it's just that their use of force is much more selective and more likely to be concealed, rather than broadcast.

Dictators care quite a bit more today about the optics. They want to appear to be legitimate, and are also actively engaged in a spin campaign about how competent they are (Guriev and Treisman, 2020). Dictators are able to manipulate information to convince or confuse the public about their abilities. If this fails to work, they can also rely on friction or, metaphorically speaking, speed bumps. By speed bumps, this means building obstacles to make it more difficult for citizens to exert their civil liberties and access information. For example, a government website that is supposed to provide transparent data will mysteriously not be working or the government can impose taxes on mobile data to make it harder to access information. True, dictators still censor and control what information citizens can access; it's just not as clear to the public that this is by design and not due to some sort of technical glitch. We'll dive into this more later.

Dictators are also more equipped to control their citizens without resorting to physical repression through the use of technology. For example, authoritarian regimes can use technology to collect more accurate information on citizens to pinpoint where dissent is taking place. Because of this, blatant and indiscriminate uses of repression to intimidate the entire citizenry are no longer necessary. Technology has enabled authoritarian regimes to be less violent but more controlling. Before exploring these developments, we first lay out how the nature of repression has changed (Guriev and Treisman, 2019). Drawing from research of the last several decades, the chapter then looks at tools of legitimation, such as pseudo-democratic institutions and propaganda, and digital tools of control.

A Different Type of Repression: Selective, Timely and Covert

Authoritarian regimes have used terror and violence against their own citizens for many years. Both terror and violence are forms of repression, and they help authoritarian regimes to enforce order and control their populations. Repression is used to punish activities that are considered subversive to the regime and to increase the costs of collective action against the regime. This can be accomplished by detaining the opposition, deterring them from challenging the state and blocking their civil liberties (Escribà-Folch, 2013).

Repression was more frequently used in the past, as dictators wanted to showcase how brutal they were. Public purges, executions and show trials were commonplace. Saddam Hussein rose to power with a very public purge of over 100 Ba'ath party members that he accused of plotting to get rid of him. Those who remained were ordered to kill their colleagues and had little choice but to remain undyingly loyal to Saddam or face the same fate. In what was formerly Zaire, Joseph Mobutu publicly hanged four Congolese who were supposedly plotting to kill him in 1966. Mobutu made sure that everyone would take notice. The day of the hanging was declared a holiday and the entire population was invited to attend. The hanging took place in the centre of a square in the capital, which was cordoned off by police. A row of open coffins was lined up in the square, making it very clear to those accused and to the spectators what was about to happen. In Yemen, the former king, Ahmad bin Yahya, had the heads of those executed hung on the branches of trees to send a clear warning (Roucek, 1962). By advertising their brutality, dictators intimidated their opponents and potential opponents. These dictators used brutal repression to send a clear message to their opponents: don't risk it. But repression can be counterproductive (see Chapter 4 for more on this) and may lead to dissent which destabilises the regime (Lichbach, 1998). For this reason, many different types of state repression by authoritarian regimes have decreased.

Changes to the type of repression

While restrictions to private and political civil liberties, such as setting curfews and placing limits on expression, association, assembly, beliefs and press freedoms are still taking place, personal integrity violations that involve the state directly threatening the life of their citizens, such as through torture or killing, are less commonly used (Davenport, 2007; Davenport and Armstrong, 2004). Here we turn to the work of Guriev and Treisman (2019) who looked at dictatorships that lasted at least five years, and compared the outcomes of those that started in the 1970s or 1980s with those that started in the 2000s to show these shifts empirically. In their study, they demonstrate that the number of state political killings (a type of physical integrity violation) has dropped since the 1980s. Of dictators who took power in the 1980s, 62 per cent had more than ten political killings per year. In comparison, for dictators who started in the 2000s, this percentage dropped to 28 per cent. For example, Cuba under Fulgencio Batista (1952–9) allegedly murdered 20,000 Cubans. Under Raúl Castro, the number of political murders per year was less than ten. Countries like Jordan and Morocco have also seen relatively low numbers of state killings per year. There are exceptions, of course – Bashar al-Assad of Syria averaged 1,500 killings per year, but this is not the norm.

The number of authoritarian leaders holding political prisoners has also fallen. Of dictators who started in the 1970s, 59 per cent held more than 1,000 political prisoners in their worst year, compared with 16 per cent that came to power in the 2000s. The same can be said of the use of torture of political prisoners. Torture was allegedly used by 96 per cent of dictators from the 1980s, compared to 74 per cent of dictators of the 2000s (Guriev and Treisman, 2019).

All of this shows us that the nature of repression has changed. Dictators may believe that too much repression is risky because it may threaten their image both at home and abroad, and cause unrest. Instead, dictators are careful to repress selectively, both in terms of who they repress and when. Additionally, engaging in political killings, large-scale detentions and torture of the opposition, may not be necessary to hold on to power.

Dictators are able to maintain their grip more effectively by confusing, frustrating and bewildering their opponents. In the sections that follow, we lay out how they do this.

Selective Repression

Authoritarian states no longer have the will, the need or the capacity to repress all their citizens. As such, large-scale indiscriminate repression is a rare occurrence, with the enormous gulags in North Korea constituting an exception. For today's dictators, targeted and selective repression is more effective and more commonly used (Dimitrov and Sassoon, 2014). Authoritarian regimes may focus only on opposition parties that pose a threat, radical opponents of the state, or those with stronger anti-regime sentiments and who are most likely to protest (Lust-Okar, 2005). These types of opponents might also be important for mobilising other citizens against the regime. By being selective with repression, this sends a message to the citizens about the risks of challenging the state. In Mexico, during the Carlos Salinas presidency (1989–94), the opposition party – the Party of the Democratic Revolution (PRD) – alleged that 250 of its members were killed by the state during Salinas's tenure (Eisenstadt, 2003).[1]

Authoritarian regimes are also careful about the timing of repression and the target. One study that looked at 60 authoritarian regimes from 1990 to 2008 argued that autocracies are less likely to repress ordinary citizens before an election, but are more likely to repress the opposition (Bhasin and Ghandi, 2013). Indeed, for the opposition, it is the month of the election that is the most violent, with opposition leaders and activists directly targeted. In Zimbabwe, violence against the opposition and their voters was rampant (Bratton and Masunugure, 2007). In particular, the biggest opposition party – the Movement for Democratic Change (MDC) – has been the target of pre-electoral violence. In 2005, tens of thousands

[1] In spite of this violence from Mexico's single party PRI regime, on average it is single-party regimes that are the least repressive (Davenport, 2007).

were displaced and hundreds were killed in what was known as Operation Murambatsvina. This made it more challenging for the opposition to mobilise before elections in subsequent contests due to fears of violence (Ploch, 2008). Similarly, in the case of Nigeria, pre-electoral violence deterred turn-out in elections in 2007 (Bratton, 2008).

Although attacks to personal integrity rights are less common, these types of human rights violations still take place against opponents of authoritarian regimes. Returning to the case of Zimbabwe, after Emmerson Mnangagwa succeeded long-time leader Robert Mugabe (1987–2017), there was initially hope that the new leadership would be less violent and repressive. However, security forces have continued to engage in abductions and torture of opposition politicians and activists. Human Rights Watch reported in 2020 that over 70 dissidents were abducted but were later released (2021). Being a member of the opposition or an activist is still a risky endeavour in authoritarian regimes.

In spite of the horrifying examples from Zimbabwe, the trend is that these risky and brazen physical integrity violations are in decline. Certainly, examples exist where this is still happening, but when looking at the big picture, dictatorships are much more selective in who they target and when, and they are more likely to target political civil liberties rather than physical integrity rights. They are also less likely to block or fully ban political civil liberties. In the section that follows, we look at what these new forms of repression look like in practice.

Speed bumps and Cumbersome Laws

As the previous section illustrated, repression still exists, but it is usually more selective – regarding who is targeted, how they are targeted, and when they are targeted. When it comes to addressing political civil liberties, the nature of repression has also changed. Authoritarian regimes want to restrict civil liberties without engaging in outright censorship and bans. They also no longer want to expunge the opposition completely, as that would attract too much negative attention from the international community, and could backfire and lead to resistance and instability. Instead, authoritarian regimes are creating speed bumps that disrupt, delay, confuse, frustrate and impede their targets, rather than block them. They are passing laws that don't annihilate the opposition, but make it harder for their opponents to function. As an example, authoritarian regimes can engage in short-term detentions that disrupt the opposition, such as placing opponents under house arrest instead of in prison. They can also deny their opponents access to jobs and educational opportunities, or prevent them from travelling by seizing their travel documents.

One of the main targets for authoritarian speed bumps are NGOs. Rather than the outright banning of NGOs, authoritarian regimes make it more difficult for them to operate. Starting from 2006 (and again in 2009 and 2012), Russia designed a series of laws to prevent NGOs from receiving foreign funding (which almost all pro-democracy NGOs do). Any organisation that engages in political activity and receives foreign funding must register with the government as a foreign agent and be subject to audits. There is also a fairly broad definition of what constitutes political activity, and groups like the Orthodox Church have been conveniently exempted. In Russia, all donations of more than $6,700 are subject to mandatory monitoring, all material used by NGOs (including information on the internet) must be labelled as a product of a foreign agent, and any organisation that violates the law is monitored by the same federal agency responsible for investigating money laundering and terrorism. The effect was that it cut the financial lifeline of NGOs based in Russia and damaged their credibility, leaving many NGOs forced to operate elsewhere, such as the MacArthur Foundation and the Committee Against Torture. Other autocratic countries, such as Hungary, have followed suit with their own laws. One study showed that between 1955 and 1994, only 17 out of 195 countries had passed more restrictive laws regarding the foreign funding of NGOs. Data from 1995 to 2012 revealed that 69 additional countries adopted legislation to restrict foreign funding, such as Uganda and Cambodia (Dupuy et al., 2015).

Authoritarian regimes also don't directly censor the media. Instead, using civil and criminal libel lawsuits is another speed bump used to muzzle the free press. In Turkey, a journalist was sued for trying to defame President Erdoğan on Twitter in May 2014. In Russia, Vladimir Putin introduced criminal liability for libel in 2012, or essentially anyone who criticises the government. Any libel prosecution that had been scrapped during the term of his predecessor, Dmitry Medvedev, was also reopened.

Cumbersome laws have also been enacted to target popular bloggers. In Russia, a blogger's law requires anyone with an online presence of more than 3,000 daily visitors to register and disclose their personal information. The government also passed a law which designated media organisations that received funding from abroad as foreign agents – and those who failed to declare would be in legal jeopardy. Another law was passed in 2017 which denied citizens anonymity in messaging services and compels ISPs (Internet Service Providers) to restrict user access to messaging platforms if the content of messages is suspected of violating Russian laws (Lonkila et al., 2021). In Saudi Arabia, citizens who want to post videos online would need to obtain a licence, and uploading a video without a licence was punishable by law (Ifteqar, 2022). Laws are in place that make it more difficult for citizens in authoritarian regimes to post their opinions freely on the internet.

Libel lawsuits are also used to silence the opposition. In Singapore, there are rules that anyone who has declared bankruptcy cannot run for public office. Libel lawsuits that force people into bankruptcy are used as a way of ensuring that the opposition cannot run, as was the case for 11 opposition leaders between 1971 and 1993. In Malaysia, former Prime Minister Mohamed silenced his critics by launching defamation suits against them (Varol, 2014).

Authoritarian regimes also don't always engage in outright censorship. Information is really only dangerous to the regime if it facilitates citizens' coordination and mobilisation (Egorov et al., 2009). Censorship can therefore be more targeted. One study noted how censorship of the internet in China only targets online content that hints at collective action to overthrow the regime (King et al., 2013).[2] Additionally, there are also certain words that could attract the attention of censors, such as Tiananmen Square or Tibet Independence (MacKinnon, 2009). While some forms of free speech are allowed, information that is critical of the government faces strict punishments. Since 2012, Chinese bloggers have been required to register with the government (King et al., 2013). Additionally, anyone who posts defamatory comments that are seen by 5,000 users could face up to three years in prison, and any citizen who publicly humiliates or invents stories online can face a criminal prosecution (Lu and Zhao, 2018). Online behaviour is governed by the Criminal Code, which makes it illegal to encourage extremist activity, incite hatred, encourage terrorist activity, insult religious people or insult the government (Howells and Henry, 2021). This isn't outright censorship, but for some the impacts are as grave.

The method of controlling free speech has also changed. Instead of blatantly blocking free speech, any critical media is either starved or sued. Critical media may not be awarded a new licence or contract, may no longer benefit from government advertising, and may face constant auditing. In the case of Hungary under Viktor Orbán, any radio station that has been critical of the regime was deprived of state advertising, with some losing 90 per cent of their revenues (Schmitz, 2021). This strategy was learned from watching Putin's economic pressure campaign on editors and journalists (Buzogány, 2017). Discriminatory use of funds can affect the media, as the public sector is often one of the biggest advertisers. This isn't the state dictating what can be said, but it silences the media nonetheless.

In Turkey, as most media corporations have a larger parent corporation, this gives the government the power to punish those parent companies with critical media subsidiaries with huge tax fines. In 2009, the Dogan Media group faced a fine of $2.5 billion for allowing critical

[2] North Korea does not have the ability to use the internet as a safety valve for citizen complaints or to identify voices of the opposition. Instead, North Korea overwhelms its citizens with blunt propaganda (Gerschewski and Dukalskis, 2018).

commentary. Although the fine was reduced to $600 million, the Dogan Group had to sell its largest newspapers and its major television station. In the case of Hong Kong, the independent media was choked from their main sources of revenue, and this has tamed the more outspoken newspapers (George, 2019).

The government may also control information by providing more support and funding for private and/or public media organisations that are loyal to the regime. In Brazil, the government in the 1980s awarded broadcasting licences to top military officers in the region. In El Salvador, two families, who are aligned with the conservative ARENA party, own the most important newspapers and their markets. In Venezuela, the pro-state media dominates the news (Cañizález 2014). The global prominence of this approach shows how effective it is in shaping hearts and minds.

As another common speed bump, rather than creating political prisoners and targeting the opposition on political grounds, authoritarian regimes can bring up fake charges of tax evasion or trumped-up charges of corruption as a way of persecuting their opponents and punishing political dissidents. Many members of the opposition have faced onerous tax audits, inspections and lawsuits. In Turkey, its largest company, the Koc Group, faced tax audits after it offered refuge to protesters who had been hit with tear gas during the protests that took place in the summer of 2013 (Karaveli, 2014). The Ministry of Finance was sent to raid the three major energy-sector companies a few weeks later. In Malawi, President Bingu wa Mutharika used the charge of corruption to imprison his opponents in 2004 and 2005 (Hall-Matthews, 2007).

Pseudo-Democratic Institutions

Although authoritarian regimes are not becoming more democratic, the boundaries between a flawed democracy and an electoral regime appear to have become blurred. In reality, authoritarian regimes are using legal mechanisms for anti-democratic ends as a way of improving their democratic credentials. Using democratic institutions also helps autocracies gain valuable information from the public, mitigate elite conflict and deal with the opposition. By using democratic institutions and turning them on their heads, this cleverly conceals undemocratic practices.

Electoral façades

Elections have become routine in contemporary autocracies. In 1970, only 59 per cent of autocracies regularly held elections (one at least every six years). Today, just a handful of autocracies *don't* hold elections. This may be somewhat surprising given that elections pose inherent risks to authoritarian regimes. We explain how, in spite of their risky nature, holding elections can prolong authoritarian rule. We then close this section with how autocracies overcome these risks through electoral manipulation.

For some authors, multi-party elections pose significant challenges to authoritarian regimes (Malesky and Schuler, 2011). Multi-party elections can help the opposition learn different tactics, help mobilise civil society and build electoral coalitions. Local elections are particularly important to the opposition because, if they perform well in large cities in the years leading up to the pivotal national elections, this helps them improve their case for winning the national election. They are able to learn the best campaign strategies, while the incentives to cooperate increase as well, such as putting forward a single candidate. The opposition can resolve collective action problems around elections, which can then increase the probability of regime change (Knutsen et al., 2017). However, holding elections does not constitute a sign that a regime is about to democratise (Brownlee, 2007).

Additionally, although elections carry some degree of risk in authoritarian regimes, on average elections prolong the regime's tenure in power (Ezrow and Frantz, 2011). When authoritarian regimes hold elections where they don't engage in obvious electoral fraud, this enhances their legitimacy both domestically and internationally (Bernhard et al., 2020). Paul Kagame and the Patriot Front (RPF) in Rwanda have had dominant electoral victories since 2003, and in recognition of this, the regime has received a steady stream of support from foreign donors (Beswick, 2011). These strong electoral wins have intimidated the opposition and solidified support among the public. The RPF was not only able survive multi-party elections, but used elections to consolidate its rule (Samset, 2011).

Elections are also used by autocracies to manage destabilising elite conflict (Boix and Svolik, 2013). Elites (such as members of the ruling party) are eager to gain access to powerful positions in the government (Magaloni, 2008). Elections serve as the most credible, fair and efficient way to spread the spoils to regime elites (Wright and Escribà-Folch, 2012). The election results show which members of the ruling party are the most popular among the public, and who is most deserving of certain portfolios and government positions. Members of the ruling party have to work hard to persuade, influence or buy off voters, which also serves the regime's interests (Lust-Okar, 2006).

As the previous example from Rwanda illustrated, elections also signal strength to the opposition and may deter challenges by opponents by demoralising them. The potential opposition may feel that opposing the regime is futile after experiencing overwhelming electoral defeats (Magaloni, 2006). Instead, the opposition may choose to be co-opted and profit from the spoils of government, such as has been the case in Jordan with the Muslim Brotherhood, which has benefitted from the Ministry of Endowment portfolio (Patel, 2015). In providing clientelistic benefits for some members of the opposition, this also keeps the opposition fragmented (Lust-Okar, 2009).

It is not just elites and the opposition that are bought off, but the public as well. Dominant parties can use patronage to easily win elections, which increases loyalty and support for the regime (Green, 2011). Elections can also help to mobilise the population through the distribution of benefits such as government spending on handouts (television sets, free healthcare, tax relief) and vote-buying schemes (Lust-Okar, 2006). This has been a common practice in Mexico under the PRI, and in Malaysia under the UMNO.

Elections also provide authoritarian regimes with an important source of information that they can use to form their policies or approach to maintaining control (Magaloni, 2006). Autocratic governments often receive inaccurate or incomplete information about how the public feels about the regime. The elite in authoritarian regimes are often reluctant to convey information that is critical of the regime, or what their true preferences are. It is also difficult for authoritarian regimes to gauge the level of public support for the regime. The results of multiparty elections provide a source of objective information about regime popularity and bases of support on one hand, and opposition strength on the other (Magaloni, 2008). Thus, by holding elections, incumbents gain information about local conditions which they can use to assess where the potential challenges are to their regime (Blaydes, 2010; Cox, 2009). Elections can be a helpful tool for gathering information, which, in the long run, makes these elections worthwhile for autocratic regimes.

Local elections are also used to better understand how local officials are doing. In the case of China, candidates at the local level who do not receive a lot of support indicate to the regime that they may be incompetent. The electoral process also promotes a constructive dialogue between citizens and local officials (Martinez-Bravo et al., 2014).

Elections may also ensure a non-violent exit for authoritarian leaders. Elections offer an alternative exit for leaders rather than having to face a coup (Cox, 2009). By the same token, dictators who come to power through elections are more likely to peacefully retire rather than face a violent ouster. In one study looking at dictators who had stepped down between 1946 and 2013, more than half of those who were not elected to power were either exiled, imprisoned or killed within one year (Guriev and Treisman, 2019). Elections hold numerous benefits for authoritarian regimes, but how do autocrats ensure that elections don't become their downfall? We spell out the tools of electoral manipulation below.

In authoritarian regimes, elections are never completely free and fair, or else they would no longer be authoritarian. However, most of today's authoritarian regimes also do not engage in blatant, massive fraud. Instead, authoritarian regimes resort to something that Andreas Schedler (2002) referred to as electoral manipulation. Authoritarian regimes can renovate the formal institutional structures to ensure that the strengths of the ruling party are captured by the electoral rules. Examples of this include manipulation of voter registration laws, candidate selection rules, and district magnitude, as well as gerrymandering, media dominance and vote buying.

Tackling voter registration laws is one way that authoritarian parties undermine suffrage. For example, in Venezuela Hugo Chávez prevented any Venezuelan citizens living in the US from voting, since they were unlikely to vote for him. In Zimbabwe, Robert Mugabe required urban residents who were more likely to oppose him to provide proof of residency. This disenfranchised these voters because many urbanites were unlikely to have proof of residency if they lived with friends or family. In other countries, voter identification laws have been used to disenfranchise ethnic minorities, who have been denied formal identification, making it impossible for them to vote. And it is not just about disenfranchising the opposition. Authoritarian regimes can also go to great lengths to ensure that loyal voters are able to vote. In the case of Russia, early voting and at home voting schemes help mobilise voters who tend to be loyal to the regime.

Authoritarian regimes can also manipulate the candidate selection and list placement, by vetting or banning certain candidates from running (Birch, 2011). Iran's theocratic regime has had a long history of holding presidential elections where the candidates were heavily vetted by the Guardian Council, an unelected body. With 585 candidates barred from running in the presidential elections of 2021, the result (a resounding victory for hard-liner Ebrahim Raisi) was a foregone conclusion.

In Russia, the party has not only blocked ballot access for the opposition to prevent strong candidates from running by refusing to certify signatures or citing procedural irregularities, but has also flooded elections with a mix of hopeless and friendly opposition (Panov and Ross, 2013; Smyth and Turovsky, 2018). Thus, there is a range of choices, which creates the appearance of competition, but all strong challengers are removed and the opposition are left fragmented. Russia learned that in regions where the opposition is the strongest, the strategy that was least likely to trigger protests is to pack the ballot, rather than barring candidates (Smyth and Turovsky, 2018). Thus, opposition parties can be excluded, subverted or fragmented.

Authoritarian regimes can also manipulate the electoral rules, such as changing the district magnitude (usually increasing the number of seats per district to benefit the biggest party), or changing the size and shape of the districts to benefit the incumbent, known as gerrymandering. The electoral threshold can also be changed to suit the incumbent, which is what happened in the case of Russia where the electoral threshold was increased from 5 per cent to 7 per cent, which suited the United Russia party, since it made it more difficult for opposition parties to meet that threshold. In Egypt, former President Hosni Mubarak changed the electoral system in 2005 so that only parties that had existed for over five years and that had at least 5 per cent of the seats in each chamber of the legislature could nominate a candidate for office. It was only Mubarak's National Democratic Party (NDP) that was able to meet this threshold, so not surprisingly the NDP dominated. Case in point, in the December 2010 parliamentary elections, the NDP secured 420 of the 508 seats available.

In addition to playing with the electoral rules, autocracies can prevent citizens from expressing their genuine preferences, known as preference distortions, either by buying citizens off or intimidating them (Schedler, 2010). To entice citizens to the polls in Bangladesh, the ruling party has offered food, free transportation to the polls, small bribes and festival events (i Coma and Morgenbesser, 2020). Russia has not yet developed this type of patronage structures, and the United Russia Party does not function as an instrument of patronage. Voter benefits are targeted to key constituencies instead, such as towards the police, the civil service and pensioners. Russia also relies heavily on collaboration with a loyal opposition whose party members are co-opted by the federal government in exchange for perks (Smyth and Turovsky, 2018). And if all of this fails, there is always voter intimidation and threats, which regimes may still rely upon to ensure a clear path to victory. Regimes with intensive patronage networks can withhold benefits to citizens who vote for opposition candidates and parties, such as has been the case in Jordan and Egypt (Blaydes, 2010; Lust-Okar, 2006). In Bangladesh, voters who don't comply with the regime may face harsh fines and disruptions of certain services (i Coma and Morgenbesser, 2020). All these strategies of electoral manipulation ensure a smooth electoral victory for authoritarian regimes, come election time.

Partisan legislatures

Another democratic institution that has become more commonly used in authoritarian regimes are legislatures, or parliaments, or other law-making bodies. In 1975, more than half of authoritarian regimes did not have any elected legislature. Forty years later, more than two-thirds had legislatures with some opposition present. Legislatures are important to authoritarian regimes because they may increase societal support for the regime by helping to legitimate it. More importantly, however, they are instruments of co-optation (Gandhi and Przeworski, 2007).

Legislatures provide credible guarantees to regime elites and to the opposition (Wright and Escribà-Folch, 2012), facilitating the distribution of patronage, particularistic rewards and perks to the opposition and access to rents (Reuter and Robertson, 2015). For example, the opposition may be given access to jobs, cars, free travel, cheap housing and/or business opportunities. Legislatures also give the opposition the opportunity to influence policy or earn policy concessions. This all lessens the likelihood that the opposition will try to mobilise protests against the regime. In doing so, this helps to reduce conflict between the party and the opposition, which helps ensure the longevity of the regime (Boix and Svolik, 2013). In fact, leaders in authoritarian regimes with a legislature are less likely to be removed from power than leaders without legislatures (Boix and Svolik, 2013).

Legislatures are also easy to control. Autocratic leaders may tightly restrict the formal powers of the legislatures; they may control, influence or appoint who is selected to be a legislator. They may also set up incentive structures to ensure that legislators cooperate either through intimidation or co-optation. Autocratic leaders can also purposely confuse or disorganise the legislative assembly by encouraging the proliferation of political parties, manipulating the legislative agenda and/or giving legislators assignments and tasks that are meaningless or non-controversial (Schedler, 2010). Authoritarian regimes can try to remove sensitive policy areas from the remit of elected officials. There are a range of tools and techniques to ensure that no real opposition emerges in the legislature.

The presence of a parliament in authoritarian regimes may also impact repression and resistance. What does this mean? Authoritarian legislatures can be used as a forum to mitigate popular discontent. This makes it less likely that the opposition will try to mobilise the public, and more likely that they will try to work out their differences with the incumbent regime through the parliament. Russia has developed a ‘pro-democracy’ website called E-Parliament, which allows Russian citizens to communicate directly with members of parliament. In reality, the website helps the Kremlin to monitor more closely the views of citizens and gives the state the opportunity to pre-empt the opposition (Meredith, 2013).

Loyal Judiciaries

Another democratic institution that authoritarian regimes can rely on to consolidate their power are judicial institutions, such as the courts. Judicial institutions serve a different purpose in autocracies; according to Thomas Ginsburg and Tamir Moustafa (2008), it is the rule *by* law, instead of the rule *of* law. Instead of interpreting the laws to protect and uphold citizens’ rights, the courts are used to establish social control and marginalise opponents. Examples abound of authoritarian regimes using the courts to serve their own purpose. The military regimes in Brazil and Chile used the courts to prosecute the various opponents to their regimes. In the Soviet Union, the military courts were given jurisdiction over political cases, while show trials under Stalin were used to intimidate opponents.

Not surprisingly, the judicial institutions in authoritarian regimes are usually not independent from the regime. Authoritarian regimes can restrict the power of the judiciary by limiting its ability to interpret the laws in controversial areas, limit their investigative powers or by refusing to enforce their decisions. They can create a parallel court system, where special courts overlap, compete and supersede the regular court system.

Judges are often carefully selected based on the leader's confidence that they either share the leaders' views or will be easily pliable. Authoritarian regimes not only control judicial appointments; they also have rules in place that make it easy to remove judges and determine the salaries of judges and their promotions based on how well they defer to the regime's interests. Judges are also socialised to believe that the judiciary needs to be depoliticised – in other words, the judiciary needs to avoid playing politics or interpreting the law based on their own moral convictions (Balasubramaniam, 2009). Singapore's judges have more autonomy from the state in theory, but in practice adhere to norms to not ever rule against the interests of the regime (Solomon, 2007). More often than not, the judiciary tries to avoid confrontation with the executive in order to protect its own autonomy and to prevent any more additional interference. Judges in authoritarian regimes often understand the limits to their power and do not challenge the regime unless they know that the regime is losing power.

Altthough the courts in autocracies do not function in the same way as they do in democracies, just like elections and legislatures, they do serve a purpose for authoritarian regimes. The courts check the power of other institutions that present a challenge to the incumbent regime. In Iran, the regime has used the unelected judicial institutions to check the elected institutions that were at times controlled by reformers. In Russia, Putin used federal courts to nullify thousands of regional laws that were not consistent with the federal constitution, helping him to consolidate his power and eliminate vertical checks coming from regional governments (Varol, 2014).

The judicial institutions have also been used to implement controversial policies or decisions that the regime would prefer to distance itself from.

In the case of Egypt, the Egyptian Supreme Constitutional Court (SCC) was used to overturn socialist-oriented policies, which would have been controversial with the public. Had the regime been made directly responsible, it would have been forced to face more direct backlash from the opposition and the public (Moustafa, 2007). Many authoritarian regimes also give more power to the courts to settle labour disputes, handle criminal prosecutions and other sensitive disputes in which it prefers to remain above the fray.

The courts are used to provide legitimacy to the regime. Maintaining an appearance of constitutional legality provided states like South Korea, Taiwan and the Philippines the veneer of adhering to the rule of law during their respective periods of dictatorship during the 1960s and 70s. In Egypt, Anwar Sadat used the rhetoric of the rule of law to overcome a legitimacy gap he suffered after the death of Nasser in 1970. Although judges in Pakistan have at times gone against the military, the courts have also repeatedly legalised the right of the military to rule after a coup (Moustafa, 2007).

The courts are also utilised in authoritarian regimes to attract external investment and trade by providing the impression that they are abiding by the rule of law. The World Trade Organization (WTO) explicitly requires governments to have some sort of judicial institutions in the area of trade in order to engage in dispute resolution and provide assurances to investors. By using the courts – and giving them autonomy over economic areas – the regime can make credible commitments that a neutral institution can monitor and punish violations of property rights.

The courts are also used to keep the administrative institutions in check, and ensure that they comply with what the regime's interests are, and maintain better discipline (Varol, 2014). The courts help to enforce order in the bureaucracy, and can provide a mechanism by which leaders can gain information on misdeeds committed by the administrative institutions. Citizens in Mexico, for example, were encouraged to use the courts to challenge bureaucrats who were not properly implementing policies. As many authoritarian regimes face high levels of corruption, judicial review can be used to give the appearance of neutrality, offering a check on corrupt administrative practices.

The courts in democracies are supposed to interpret the laws and defend the rule of law and various freedoms. The courts work at the behest of the country and its citizens. In authoritarian regimes, the courts are used to support the regime and control its citizens. The courts exist, but have very different functions. The same can be said of the fake NGOs created by autocracies that impersonate real NGOs, but have little democratic function.

Fake NGOs

Authoritarian regimes have also taken note of the work of NGOs, particularly those that have formed to support democracy. NGOs are important to fostering awareness of the rights of individuals to exercise freedoms of expression, assembly and association. They also highlight where corruption and human rights violations are taking place. To counter the threat of pro-democracy NGOs, which mushroomed in new democracies after the Cold War ended (Dupuy et al., 2015), authoritarian regimes have created their own government-organised non-governmental organisations (GONGOs). GONGOs can perform numerous tasks, including zombie election monitoring and providing propaganda. While some GONGOs have benign objectives, others are formed with the main goal of subverting debate, spreading lies, confusing the public and crowding out democratic voices. Examples include Saudi Arabia's International Islamic Relief Organization and the Myanmar Women's Affairs Federation, which have masqueraded as human rights and women's rights NGOs.

In China, all domestic, cultural, economic and social organisations must establish party-based groups, called PONGOs, which enable the regime to exercise even greater control over collective activity. Chinese GONGOs were used to attend a Universal Periodic Review session to intimidate and threaten democratic activists and drown out any accusations of human rights violations. GONGOs from Russia, Kazakhstan,

Azerbaijan and Belarus have attended the OSCE's Human Dimension Implementation Meetings (HDIMs). During these meetings, the GONGOs directly confronted independent civil society groups to sow confusion about Russia's 2014 invasion of Ukraine. At a Summit of the Americas in 2015, Venezuelan and Cuban GONGOs conflicted with authentic civil society groups to confuse and contradict their activities. At the UNHRC meetings, at least two-thirds or more of the NGOs are actually GONGOs. GONGOs are allowed to flourish, while authoritarian regimes have cracked down on independent NGOs.

In addition to fake NGOs, there are also fake protest movements. In the case of Russia, Facebook pages were developed to support anti-revolutionary rallies in response to the Orange Revolution in Ukraine. Websites were also established ostensibly by the government to pay off participants to attend pro-Putin rallies (Meredith, 2013).

Fake institutions, fake NGOs and fake protest movements are all part and parcel for authoritarian regimes. Autocracies want to appear to be democratic not just for the optics but because all of this effort to mimic democracies actually serves a purpose – namely, it prolongs authoritarian rule. Authoritarian regimes have figured out how to pervert democratic institutions to their advantage. They have also figured out how to use spin to enhance their image. We explain in more detail what we mean in the following section.

Spin Dictators

Authoritarian regimes have not only turned democratic institutions into instruments of political survival, but they have also mimicked democracies in how they communicate. For example, autocracies now use a similar type of rhetoric as democrats, such as boasting about economic performance.[3] True, the use of propaganda is not necessarily new (as totalitarian regimes have used mass communication to assert control over

[3]While democratically elected leaders are ironically using the language of foreign threats and enemies.

their populations (see Friedrich and Brzezinski, 1956). Nevertheless, there has been a renewed interest in looking at the role of propaganda in sustaining authoritarian regimes and how the use of propaganda may differ from the past (Guriev and Treisman, 2019, 2020). In China, exposure to the mass media has made citizens less critical of the regime and the political system (Stockmann and Gallagher, 2011). Although authoritarian regimes may allow some free media to check the effectiveness of local governments and institutions, the media is mostly used to provide uncritical, and at times, laudatory content (Egorov et al., 2009).

One of the most notable differences are the mediums of communication. Although there are still traditional mediums of propaganda such as print campaigns, films, television and radio shows, etc., the internet has changed the way in which dictatorships spin narratives. To be certain, the internet has facilitated authoritarian regimes' abilities to broadcast their propaganda and criticise their opponents. To quote Rød and Weidmann (2015), the internet is the 'modern version of the capillary through which the blood of the dictatorship diffuses through society' (p. 341).

For autocrats, social media has been an especially effective tool to communicate with their supporters in a more personalised and immediate fashion. In Venezuela, Hugo Chávez used social media to boast about how much popular support there was for his socialist vision (Waisbord and Amado, 2017). Former Ecuadoran President Rafael Correa, who was followed by almost 7 per cent of the population, regularly tweeted derogatory tweets about the media and the opposition (ibid.). In El Salvador, President Nayib Bukele regularly uses Twitter to address citizens about the accomplishments and directives of the government, with *The Economist* running a story about him titled 'My Tweet is Your Command' (Esberg, 2020). Social media is used by autocrats to directly connect with their citizens and tout their successes with minimal effort.

The internet has also been useful to authoritarian regimes to inundate their citizens with massive amounts of information – also known as flooding, a form of digital authoritarianism (digital authoritarianism will be discussed in detail in the next section). Flooding constitutes a third-generation strategy of censorship. Past strategies of censorship involved direct forms of censorship that included blocking a specific website. Today, autocracies deal with potential threats to their regimes through effective counter-information campaigns that overwhelm, discredit and demoralise opponents. Essentially, the government produces information to distract and confuse citizens on sensitive political issues, which pre-empts any potential criticism of the regime. Regimes can flood social media with information that is supportive of the regime or demonises the opposition (Roberts, 2018). China hired thousands of bloggers to write supportive pieces about the regime, such as praising a successful government project, while in Russia, independent hackers were hired to troll and hinder the communication of the opposition. In Uganda, there are over 440 Twitter accounts that spread pro-government propaganda (Fröhlich, 2022). Authoritarian regimes can use automated bots and troll armies to harass critics, spread misinformation, and erode trust in independent media outlets. By doing so, this provides plausible deniability for the use of censorship, propaganda and repression. This also can ultimately confuse people. If there is an onslaught of propaganda to convince the public of something, it makes it even harder for citizens to discern what is false and what is the truth. Russia and China are expert at using bots and trolls to provide a relentless flood of information.

In looking at Russian internet users, it was estimated that only 7 per cent were recognisable humans, while the remaining 93 per cent were news accounts, bots, hybrid or anonymous (Kurowska and Reshetnikov, 2018b). Russian trolls are not arguing in favour of one political position to transform the preferences of the Russian public. Instead, they are flooding citizens with an overabundance of conflicting opinions to confuse and disorient, a process known as neutrollisation (Kurowska and Reshetnikov, 2018a). As citizens realise that their engagement is futile, since the internet is filled with absurd fabrications and red herrings, this may lead more to disillusionment and apathy, which discourages political mobilisation before it can materialise (Kurowska and Reshetnikov, 2018b). Russia's strategy is not about brainwashing as much as it is about disorienting.

China has also effectively used the internet to manipulate, confuse, divide, repress, disorient and entertain. The CCP also uses social media platforms such as Weibo, WeChat and LeTV to increase internal and external ideological propaganda. Fake social media posts to disrupt discussion of controversial topics, generate about 448 million fake comments every year (Tucker et al., 2017). Twitter had to suspend more than 200,000 fake accounts that had been set up by the Chinese government to spread misinformation during the protests in Hong Kong in 2019. The Chinese government distorts facts, changing narratives, and deliberately guiding people to forget history (Qiang, 2021). By using algorithms and bots to mislead the public, this enhances the effectiveness of its propaganda machine.

But it's not just Russia and China that use digital tools of manipulation. Under President Rodrigo Duterte in the Philippines, a small army of digital strategists, bloggers and influencers were used to distract and confuse the public, and harass and discredit any political opponents. Duterte has flooded social media with disinformation and attacks against journalists, politicians and human rights activists. The government has also made use of fake grass-roots efforts, known as 'astro-turfing', to multiply the number of messages in support of the regime from a group of patriotic trolls who have created numerous online identities (Lamensch, 2021). Many authoritarian states have bot armies and fake news websites that use digital automation or fabrication tools to give the impression of popular support. State-run media and the state more generally encourage social media mobs and individual influencers who are pro-regime (Qiang, 2021).

Authoritarian regimes care about their image. They go to great lengths to craft their image and offer an onslaught of information about how wonderful their regimes are. With the spread of the internet, it is inevitable that citizens in autocracies are exposed to negative stories about the regime. To deal with this, authoritarian regimes have used the internet to their advantage. Online armies can dump information that is laudatory or confusing about the regime to distract from online opponents. Additionally, autocracies don't solely focus on scare tactics; they like to boast of their performance. Of course, other important tactics are needed as well, which we will explore in the next section.

The rise of digital authoritarianism

Initially, some scholars felt that the rise of the internet would liberate people in authoritarian regimes – referred to as 'liberation technology' – by spreading information that would be critical of authoritarian rule, exposing citizens to scandals and corruption, and also to democratic values and ideals. Information could be more easily exchanged, and the political agenda of the opposition would be easier to access. Scholars noted that in the case of the Arab Spring, in particular, the internet played a key role in facilitating the protests and overcoming collective action problems (El Baradei, 2011). The following chapter will explain in greater detail the role of social media in facilitating protest and democratic change.

Although these technological improvements have helped facilitate the spread of information, technology is increasingly used to repress, and authoritarian regimes have become savvier at using technology to surveil, harass and manipulate their populations. Taken together, this is known as digital authoritarianism, or *repression technology* (Boas, 2006). And repression technology seems to be working in favour of authoritarian regimes. A study demonstrated that authoritarian regimes that use digital forms of repression are the most durable (Kendall-Taylor et al., 2020). Why might this be the case? More specifically, it lowers the chances of protest and other destabilising events. For example, Cambodia created a Cyber War team in 2014 to monitor the internet and flag anti-government activity, and saw the number of protests go down (ibid.).

In some authoritarian regimes, improvements have been made in artificial intelligence, such as facial recognition technology and algorithms that closely monitor citizen behaviour, while internet firewalls have shut down what information is available and limited the competition of ideas. China in particular has developed extensive legal and technical abilities to monitor and regulate online activity, and to censor and surveil its own citizens.[4] Access to internet data on blog posts, Twitter updates, photos and videos yields not only useful information on individuals, but important intelligence on broad social trends (Meredith, 2013). While the previous section focused more on how technology is used to manipulate, confuse and brainwash citizens, in this section we focus on how authoritarian regimes use technology to spy on their citizens, and block and disrupt the flow of information.

Surveillance

In contrast to the past, where regimes relied on a massive surveillance system that was equipped with a human army of secret police (like the Stasi in East Germany) and citizen informants, today's autocrats are even more intrusive with the help of technology that offers new opportunities for surveillance, which is easier to disguise (Blaydes, 2018). Citizens transmit all sorts of information through the internet that can be surveilled by the government. Autocracies use machine learning techniques, spying malware and automated mass-detection systems to identify government critics (Gohdes, 2014, 2020). All of these tools are used to track online activity and contain threats before they spread (Qin et al., 2017). Additionally, surveillance cameras and facial-recognition technology make it easier for autocracies to identify opponents and monitor early signs of protest (Zeng, 2020).

In Iran and Syria, improvements in technology have been used to digitally surveil citizens, especially those who are considered to be threatening to the regime (Gohdes, 2014; Gunitsky, 2015). In Ethiopia, surveillance is facilitated by the widespread use of mobile phones. Personal information and a photograph must be submitted by customers when purchasing a SIM card. Once the SIM card is activated, the phone is easy to monitor, and every phone call and SMS message can be accessed by the government.

[4] China's country-wide cybersecurity spending in 2019 was estimated at $7.35 billion, with the government accounting for about 60% of total expenditures (Xinhua, 2019).

Mobile phone access can also be blocked during politically tense or sensitive moments (Ayalew, 2021). In Venezuela, Chávez was able to use technology to identify several million voters who voted against him in 2004. Those who were identified by Chávez as opponents of the regime faced retribution and saw a 5 per cent drop in earnings (Hsieh et al., 2011).

Russia has also built the Systems for Operative Investigative Activities (SORM), which intercepts telephone and internet communications. Initially implemented in Russia in 1995, Belarus, Kyrgyzstan and Kazakhstan have followed suit in 2010, 2012 and 2018, respectively. Russia has also targeted civil society groups with surveillance, and used the information gathered to find ways to harass and punish them. Surveillance of different websites enabled the government to investigate which websites to shut down, such as a website dedicated to supporting miners and their families after a mine exploded and 99 people died in May 2010.

The gold standard for surveillance technology goes to China, however. Since the early 1990s, China's Ministry of Public Security (MPS) has carried out the National Public Security Work Informational Project, also called the Golden Shield Project, which is a security management information system, a criminal information system and a national adult citizens database. Additionally, to monitor its citizens, the country is covered in millions of surveillance cameras, while laws allow total surveillance of citizens' online activities. A Skynet system, which was first established in 2003, is in place to connect surveillance cameras from different locations to be able to identify a large number of people quickly. Launched in 2005, Skynet boasted 800,000 cameras in Beijing alone, totally covering the capital by 2015 (Polyakova and Meserole, 2019).

Meanwhile, the Sharp Eyes Project was implemented to provide complete real-time rural surveillance coverage by building high-definition cameras at main road entrances and crowd-gathering places in rural areas. Sharp Eyes also places surveillance capabilities in citizens' hands and encourages their direct participation so that there is full range coverage and full network sharing. Along with high resolution cameras, China also uses facial recognition technology to track citizens' online activities to contain potential threats (Qin et al, 2017). With face recognition technology, Chinese authorities can quickly access an individual, and Chinese police can be immediately deployed at locations where an individual's face has been captured.

Sensor data and artificial intelligence tracking around the country makes surveillance omnipresent. While this affects all Chinese citizens, nowhere is this more oppressive than for the Uighurs in north-west China. The Uighur population is constantly being monitored, living in what has been referred to as a 'digital gulag' (Feay, 2019). They are identified through facial recognition, while their smartphones are tracked to determine their whereabouts. This is not by choice. Uighurs are required to download apps on their phones that allow the authorities to monitor what they look at and track their movements (Qiang, 2021). Uighurs must provide DNA samples, or have their voices recorded so that authorities can use speech-recognition tools when spying on their phone conversations (Lamensch, 2021).

Websites like Weibo and WeChat are closely monitored, and dissidents and human rights activists are frequently detained for posting any information that is considered to be threatening. Any website that does not comply with the government's standards is shut down. In the first few weeks of 2019, over 700 websites and 9,000 mobile phone apps were closed down (Xu, 2021).

Today's authoritarian regimes have access to much more sophisticated technology. For regimes like China, they can use technology to monitor dissidents, which requires only targeted types of repression (Xu, 2021).

Friction and Censorship

In addition to spying on their own citizens, authoritarian regimes can also make it more difficult for information to flow, known as 'friction' (as the chapter earlier explained, this is a type of speed bump). Beyond the common practice of shutting down traffic to specific websites, sophisticated technology exists for filtering unwanted content, such as by selectively removing search results, removing social media posts or simply just slowing down the internet (see Roberts, 2018). There are numerous ways in which regimes can use friction to their advantage. Regimes can make it more difficult to access government information that is important for publicising government failures. They can create fees for accessing information that should be free of charge to access. Governments can cause delay in accessing information, but journalists and citizens may not even realise that they are being affected. In Ethiopia, although most television and radio stations are government owned, the regime can also jam signals to prevent any controversial content from airing (Grinberg, 2017).

The timing of censorship is also important. Authoritarian regimes increasingly block websites just before important political events, such as demonstrations. In Iran, at the height of the 2009 election protests, the Iranian government brought down the websites of the Green Movement supporters by using distributed denial-of-service attacks (Michaelsen, 2018). Shutting down the internet or certain websites is also a common practice in some African autocracies. Uganda, Burundi, Ethiopia, Chad and the Republic of Congo all interrupted access to the internet during their electoral periods (Freyburg and Garbe, 2018). When Zimbabwe's ruling party, the Zimbabwe African National Union-Patriotic Front (ZANU-PF), was going through a noted period of intense internal fighting, two notable internet shutdowns took place. The first was a partial closure of WhatsApp in July 2016 for four hours, and the second was the total closure of all internet services for at least seven days in January 2019 (Mare, 2020). Based on Article 64, Russia blocked mobile data service in Ingushetia after there was regional arrest and calls for separatism in 2018. Other mass protests that took place in 2018 in Chechnya also led to a blackout of three mobile service providers on behalf of state security agencies. Similar measures took place in Moscow in response to protests in the summer of 2019 (Shahbaz and Funk, 2019).

There are very few autocracies around the world where the population can freely use the internet, such as in Malaysia and Singapore (Rød and Weidmann, 2015). Some authoritarian regimes are not selective in their censorship at all. In North Korea, where many people do not have access to the internet, there is no access to alternative information, with exceptions made to co-opt powerful loyalists who may need to use internet access for their own businesses (Gerschewski and Dukalskis, 2018). Saudi Arabia only had a single gateway through which Saudi citizens could access outside information. Access to the internet was delayed until the regime had the capacity to filter information, which informed users that the content of a certain website was forbidden (Kalathil and Boas, 2003).

China also has unprecedented levels of control over the internet, which is overseen by over 60 agencies working together, reporting directly to Xi Jinping since 2014.[5] The Chinese government censors and monitors content, and blocks and suppresses any content that inspires collective action, while trying to make people feel as though they are free to express themselves. China had an early start in blocking information from the internet. China's internet governance system, known informally as the Great Firewall (GFW), was created in 1996 by the State Council Order 195. It was constructed by 50 governing bodies that were responsible for implementing over 200 policies. The Firewall has choke points that enable the state to block servers and sites across the country and control internet access on a national and regional level. The Firewall can block foreign websites and platforms like Twitter, Google, Facebook and YouTube, as well as virtual private networks (VPNs). The GFW surveils, intercepts and blocks internet transmissions according to the official requirements of the CCP. It also blocks foreign internet tools and mobile apps, and forces foreign companies to adapt to domestic regulations. China also relies on applications that employ thousands of people engaged in manual censorship to remove content that violates China's strict laws (Qiang, 2019).

Although Russia does not have the technological capacity to filter all the information that its citizens receive (and must rely more on intimidating civil society), the government has passed a series of laws and has blocked

[5]The Cyberspace Administration of China (CAC), which has been responsible for Internet governance since 2014, answers directly to China's State Council, which Xi Chairs (Creemers, 2016; Lu and Zhao, 2018)

technology that would allow for the free flow of information. In 2017, Russia passed a law that gave the authorities a huge mandate to block online content that it deemed undesirable or extremist (Morgus, 2019). Although difficult to enforce, this leads to greater levels of self-censorship. In Russia, there are also complex, but ultimately highly restrictive speech and expression laws that are designed to deter free speech (Polyakova and Meserole, 2019).

In the Middle East, there are similarly harsh laws on free speech on sensitive topics. In Jordan, an Anti-Terror Law was passed in 2014, which could be used to prosecute internet users who are critical of the Gulf states and their monarchies on social media (Human Rights Watch, 2014). This has led to actual arrests and prison sentences of Jordanian nationals who have been accused of criticising the United Arab Emirates. A Saudi citizen, Abdulrahman al-Sadhan who criticised the kingdom on Twitter, was tracked down and disappeared for several years, and was then sentenced to 20 years in prison (Kirchgaessner, 2021).

The Russian government also went after social media apps and private networks.[6] In 2018, the Russian government blocked Telegram, the social media app that is similar to WhatsApp. The Russian internet regulator had to block 18 million IP addresses, which disrupted banking, transport and news sites (Roth, 2018). Since 2017, Russia has also blocked virtual private networks (VPNs) that allow access to banned content.

In addition to passing restrictive laws and blocking social media apps, authoritarian regimes can also surveil citizens and censor information through third-party intermediaries. Most online service providers in authoritarian regimes are provided by state-run telecommunication agencies, such as in Belarus and Iran. These agencies are connected to personal computers and can monitor the traffic generated by the computers and their subscribers. If the online service provider is not state-owned, an authoritarian government can also dictate to telecommunications companies and other third-party intermediaries, such as internet access providers, search engines and social networking sites, to censor information. This has increased the opportunities

[6] In Russia, approximately 76% of the population by the end of 2018 had access to the internet (Shahbaz & Funk, 2019).

for censorship by proxy (MacKinnon et al., 2015). By targeting the third-party intermediaries, this can result in even stricter controls than those from the government directly. In Thailand after the military staged another coup in May 2014, the Norwegian telecommunications company Telenor was ordered to censor content (Rød and Weidmann, 2015).

In the case of Russia, internet service and telecommunications providers (ISPs) in Russia are licensed by a Russian Federal Agency, referred to as Roskomnadzor, and they are required to install the SORMs, a black box that intercepts communications traffic. This allows the FSB to seize private data from citizens without having to provide information or a warrant to the ISP itself (Soldatov and Borogan, 2017). The ISPs can then be used to block or filter content and deter users from uploading sensitive content (Howells and Henry, 2021). This is yet another obstacle in Russia that makes it more difficult for Russian citizens to exert their civil liberties.

Authoritarian regimes disrupt the flow of some information, but are much more selective about what they choose to censor and how. This is partly due to changes in the mediums of expression and communication. Authoritarian regimes of the past monitored every piece of literature, journal and newspaper article, and even works of art, operas and ballets (Wallach, 1991). Today, as the focus is on the internet, artificial intelligence can be used to filter and block content that is unfavourable to the regime, rather than relying on human censors (Kendall-Taylor et al., 2020). Additionally, most authoritarian regimes also understand that they don't need to censor everything and everyone. Although there are still some regimes like Saudi Arabia and North Korea that haven't followed suit with this trend, almost all authoritarian regimes (including China) use censorship more strategically and selectively. There are also plenty of regimes like Belarus and Mozambique that don't even have the capacity to digitally repress everything.

Conclusion

As this chapter has illustrated, authoritarian regimes function differently from the way they did in the past. They no longer appear to be fully authoritarian, but this does not mean that regimes are becoming more democratic. Instead, they just look more democratic, while remaining more durable than ever. Authoritarian regimes are cagier about their autocratic nature. Occasionally, spectacular shows of force still take place, but the target of force is only dissenters, which represent a small minority of the public. Authoritarian regimes are more careful not to engage in actions that would create moral outrage and draw international and domestic condemnation. Martial law, curfews, mass arrests and executions are used less frequently. Most citizens do not experience state brutality. That being said, although authoritarian regimes are less brutal, they are not any less controlling. Autocracies today are more at odds with human rights associated with the right to privacy and mental integrity.

However, this level of control over society can take its toll on its citizens and accumulate resentment over time. Sometimes, just one case of excessive use of force on an innocent victim can go viral, stir up outrage and galvanise people to take to the streets. In the following chapter, we will explore what citizens in authoritarian regimes can do when they have had enough.

what should we do about authoritarian regimes?

- Protest movements, authoritarian breakdown and reform.
- Response to resistance movements from authoritarian regimes.

The biggest mystery around authoritarian rule is what can be done about it. In cases where authoritarian leadership is illegitimate, corrupt and, even worse, dangerous to its own people and the outside world, is there any way to respond? Do these regimes have an Achilles heel? Studies that have investigated dealing with authoritarian regimes have not been sanguine about the probability that domestic resistance will lead to a regime being toppled, and are even less optimistic about the chances of resistance movements leading to meaningful reform. The vast majority of the time, protest movements are squashed with force. In spite of this, what are the factors that make domestic resistance most effective? Are social movements able to harness technology to their advantage when dealing with authoritarian regimes? This chapter explores the answers to these questions.

Protests movements, Resistance, Revolution and Repression

Just as the number of autocracies has been increasing around the world, so too has the number of protests. Some of the largest protests in world history have taken place in the last decade. In 2019, citizens in 20 democracies and 24 authoritarian regimes and hybrid regimes protested against rising levels of authoritarianism (Varieties of Democracy, 2020). Protests have taken place in Algeria, Sudan, Haiti, Hong Kong, Bolivia, Nicaragua and Venezuela, to name a few. In some cases, protesters ask for small democratic reforms; in other cases, protesters aim for the removal of an autocratic leader; there are also instances where the citizenry is fed up and is hoping for full regime change and a transition to democracy.

One of the more notable protests of 2022 took place in Iran. The spark was the death of 22-year-old Mahsa Amini, who died in hospital in Tehran from suspicious circumstances after the morality police arrested her for not wearing her hijab correctly. Contrary to reports by the Iranian government, Amini was no political activist. Hailing from a Kurdish family, she had intended to study law, but avoided any involvement in politics, according to friends and family. The news moved quickly about her death, outraging the general public. Anti-government protests spread across the country, even in more traditional and conservative cities such as Qom and Mashhad. Frustrations with the regime had been mounting since hardliner Ebrahim Raisi became president in 2021. The regime had also been ramping up the policing of women's dress, while the promises of the Islamic revolution failed to deliver anything other than corruption, inflation, unemployment, inequality, economic despair and global isolation. As the chapter will explain later, the regime has responded with brutal force.

In fact, for the most part, the vast majority of protests that take place in authoritarian regimes are not successful in achieving their objectives, and even fewer lead to regime change. However, there have been some notable counter-examples that have seen citizens pressure for positive change and oust autocratic leadership. Varieties of Democracy (2020) reported in 2019 that 44 per cent of all countries experienced pro-democracy protests, with 22 countries able to push for meaningful reforms. We first look at how protests spread, why these protest movements form in authoritarian regimes, in what instances they are successful and what obstacles they face.

How protests spark and spread

Not much is understood about what causes a revolution (a possible end-point of protests), as revolutions have been particularly hard to predict and regimes can collapse suddenly with little warning (Goldstone, 2001). Along the same lines, we also do not know what will cause a specific event to trigger protests in one country but not another. However, protests tend to ebb and flow over time. Protests are also more likely to be successful (regardless of their aims) when they are part of a global cycle of protest and when the grievances articulated resonate with society. To clarify, by protests, we are referring to an organised (and/or unorganised) social movement that challenges authority and aims to enact political change (Jasper and Goodwin, 2011), which includes changes to policy, institutions and regime change. Protests are a form of participation that are especially important when more traditional methods of exercising vertical accountability, such as voting, are absent (Thyen and Gerschewski, 2018). A protest cycle constitutes protests that take place at a similar time, with similar demands and characteristics (Tarrow, 1998).

Protest cycles are important because protests may have a demonstration effect, which helps them spread. What this means is that reports of protests can provoke more protests and thus spread political instability (Hale, 2019). Proponents of this view argue that transnational activists can provide information to other activists to facilitate these protests and offer strategic support, which facilitates contagion (Bunce and Wolchik, 2006). For example, the Colour Revolutions took place over a longer time interval (roughly during the early and mid-2000s) and involved countries mostly from the former Soviet Union and Eastern Europe, such as Ukraine, Georgia, Kyrgyzstan and Serbia. The activists of the Georgian

Rose Revolution were trained by the Serbian opposition group Otpor! that had organised the Bulldozer Revolution. The activists in the Orange Revolution in Ukraine also received support from the groups involved in the Rose Revolution. Thus, activists in neighbouring countries can provide the push needed to help organise protests that otherwise would not occur (Weyland, 2012). Proximity increases people's awareness of previous protests because it influences how much individuals interact with one another, the likelihood that they share a common language and consume similar media (Gleditsch and Ward, 2006). Thus, when the world is experiencing a protest cycle, dictatorships are more likely to face unrest.

The Arab Spring, for example, was part of a notable protest cycle in 2011, with a random event sparking a host of other protests in the region. The Arab Spring involved countries across North Africa and the Middle East, and spread over a shorter time-span compared to the Colour Revolutions. Events were organised along similar themes and most of the protests took place in central squares starting in December 2010 and into the months of early 2011 (Patel, 2014).

The Arab Spring really came as a surprise to many regional experts, as the Middle East was considered to be one of the most authoritarian regions in the world (and remains the case today), with very few protests and low levels of political participation. Civil society was also underdeveloped and frequently faced repression. And while there may have been grievances about repressive rule, corruption, rising costs of living and high unemployment, there were very few political opportunities or openings to protest. But an unpredictable event served as the catalyst after Tunisian fruit vendor Mohamed Bouazizi set himself on fire after the police harassed him for not having a vendor permit (having already endured many years of police harassment). Bouazizi's act of self-immolation would lead to public outrage followed by protests that then spread from Tunisia to Algeria, to the Gulf, to Egypt, to Syria, to Libya and elsewhere. The key factor was that Tunisia's security apparatus sided with the public, ousting longtime leader Zine El Abidine Ben Ali in a relatively peaceful revolution.

What triggers protests?

In spite of the difficulty in predicting revolutions, there are common triggers of regime-ending protests. In addition to the publicised death of an innocent individual (like Amini or Bouazizi), which can serve as the catalyst or spark to widespread protests, the most common triggers include a fraudulent election or an attempt by a leader to unconstitutionally extend their time in office, and/or an economic crisis that generates widespread economic hardship (Brancati and Lucardi, 2019). These triggers fall into the grievance-based approach for understanding revolutions (Jasper and Goodwin, 2011). For example, in Algeria after long-time leader Abdelaziz Bouteflika announced his candidacy for a fifth presidential term in February 2019, massive protests broke out, forcing his resignation on 2 April of that year. In Sudan, demonstrations broke out in December 2018 in response to deteriorating economic conditions and the regime tripling the price of bread. These protests continued into early 2019 until the military overthrew President Omar Bashir in April, nine days after Bouteflika resigned. Immediately following Bashir's ousting, protesters in Sudan demanded that civilian leadership take over. Both sets of protesters tried to ally with the military, chanting 'the army and the people are brothers' in Algeria and 'the army and the people are one' in Sudan.

It's hard to predict which factors will be more important in triggering regime-ending protests. Economic hardship may persist for years, and no effective protests take place. Robert Mugabe led Zimbabwe for decades and had plunged the country – which was once referred to as the breadbasket of Africa – into economic despair. Thousands of Zimbabweans protested corruption, inflation, a complete lack of public services and high unemployment in July 2016. However, it wasn't until Mugabe fired his Vice President, Emmerson Mnangagwa (who would eventually succeed Mugabe), and tried to name his second wife, Grace as his successor in October 2017, that the military finally stepped in to oust him (Beardsworth et al., 2019). Similarly, Burkina Faso experienced years of economic hardship and poverty under the leadership of Blaise Compaoré, but it was not until he attempted to change the constitution to enable himself to run for office again in 2014 that serious riots and protests broke out that led to the military forcing him to resign (Eizenga and Villalón, 2020).

Sometimes it is economic factors that trigger protests after years of repression and undermining the integrity of elections. In the case of Sri Lanka, though the regime had dissolved the parliament and postponed elections in 2020, mass protests didn't break out until March 2022 over the state of the economy. By that point, the country faced a severe economic crisis which included inflation, food and fuel shortages, and daily blackouts. Protesters called for the resignation of Sri Lankan leader Gotabaya Rajapaksa and other family members, who held key positions in the country. Rajapaksa responded by declaring a temporary state of emergency and giving security forces unprecedented power to arrest and detain citizens. This only served to escalate the violence, and in July of that year, protesters stormed the president's office, forcing Rajapaksa to flee the country (Jayasinghe et al., 2022).

In the Philippines, dictator Ferdinand Marcos faced over two years of sustained non-violent protests due to high levels of corruption, economic mismanagement and repression. Fraudulent elections on 7 February 1986 were the last straw, and a rebel group from the military, called the Reform the Armed Forces Movement (RAM), tried to stage a coup on the 22nd of February, which was thwarted by Marcos once it was discovered. But the peaceful People Power protest movement didn't relent. Non-violent protesters led by nuns and priests interrupted the regime's effort to stamp down on the coup to oust Marcos by physically placing themselves between the coup plotters and approaching tanks (Jarenpanit, 2015). Over the next few days, two million people came out to protest. By the 25th of February, Marcos was forced to flee the country and live in exile in Hawaii.

Protests in Iran have been a fairly common occurrence both before its 1978–9 revolution and after. When the headscarf was made compulsory in 1983, protests broke out against this law and have continued sporadically ever since in response to the policing of social restrictions. However, two of the more notable protest movements in Iran were sparked by electoral fraud and economic crisis. In 2009, protests broke out when presidential elections saw conservative leader Mahmoud Ahmadinejad elected, after more moderate candidates were barred from running, and there were blatant irregularities in the vote counting. The fraud was considered so outrageous that Prime Minister Mir Hossein Mousavi and former Speaker of the Parliament Mehdi Karroubi, resigned in disgust, joining the opposition. The movement focused not on regime overhaul, but on improving the fairness and legitimacy of elections. In spite of the more limited goals, the regime responded with repression, killing up to 72 individuals and arresting over 4,000.

When are protests more likely to lead to authoritarian breakdown?

As the chapter has explained, protests take place all over the world but rarely lead to success, whether aiming for reforms or authoritarian breakdown. However, there are some factors that increase the likelihood of success. One of the factors that is important is the size and the intensity of the protests. Protests that have mobilised large numbers of people can persuade holdouts to join the winning team and generate a sense of inevitability. However, in looking at protests that took place from 1989 to 2011, almost two-thirds attracted less than 10,000 participants at their single largest rally, with most ending in three days or less (Brancati, 2016: 28). For protests to be successful, according to one study, 3.5 per cent of the population would need to protest during the peak of a protest movement (Chenoweth, 2021). In the case of Russia, which has seen thousands of protesters against the war in Ukraine in 2022, this is nowhere near the almost 5 million that would be needed to meet that threshold. Other authors also argue that momentum is also important, measured by the number of participants and the concentration of dissident activity, or the interaction of the size of the movement and velocity (Chenoweth and Belgioioso, 2019). What this means is that it is not just the number of protesters, but also the number of protest activities. For example, protesters in Serbia came out en masse against Slobodan Milošević after fraudulent elections in 2000, and also stormed the parliament, overwhelming the security forces.

Another important factor is the nature of the movement, or whether it is non-violent or violent. The vast majority of studies argue that non-violent movements have the best chance of achieving their objectives (Chenoweth et al., 2011). This holds for all types of regimes (democratic, hybrid and authoritarian). A study of 149 countries between 1977 and 2002 found that regimes are less likely to respond to non-violent protest activity with repression (Carey, 2010). Another study from 2008 which looked at 320 uprisings found that non-violent movements are twice as effective in achieving their goals as violent uprising, and succeed more than half the time (Chenoweth et al., 2011). Because non-violent movements are less likely to face repression, they will find it easier to recruit participants (ibid.). Non-violent movements also impose higher costs on the incumbent regime to repress because this undermines the legitimacy of the regime to the public and the world. Protests provide clear signals that barriers to mobilisation can be overcome (Kuran, 1991).

Another related factor is the role of women in a protest movement which tends to go hand in hand with peaceful movements. As non-violent movements are also more inclusive, they are more likely to involve women, while protests that involve women are more likely to be peaceful, because women are less likely to engage in violence and more likely to ensure that the movement maintains its non-violent stance. Because of this, protests involving women are more likely to be successful and resilient. However, it is also because women engage in creative and diverse tactics (such as naming and shaming policemen in Sudan) that enables them to make an impact. In fact, one study noted that almost all major resistance movements to win independence or to topple an autocratic government featured women in important roles – providing food, shelter, intelligence, funds or other supplies (Chenoweth and Marks, 2022). Women are also more likely to encourage an inclusive strategy for recruiting other activists, which makes the movement more diverse and effective. This is particularly important because movements need to recruit a steady flow of individuals in order to be successful. Women are also more likely to help shift the loyalties of elites or other pillars of support that are needed to defect because, in many cases, women make a movement seem more legitimate (the same can be said for non-violent movements).

Drawing from the previous point, the success of a movement is also related to how close a movement is to elites or pillars of support for the regime. A campaign where protesters have some proximity to key pillars of support for the regime is critical because the protest movement can gain access to intelligence about the likelihood of defection, how loyal they are to the regime and if this loyalty is starting to waver. Proximity also means that the movement may be more capable of persuading these targets to defect, or they can cause significant disruption to their daily lives – through boycotts or strikes, for example, making defection a likely option.

Added to this, the other important factor in the success of a protest movement is the role of elites. The most prominent theories of authoritarian breakdown argue that the elites hold the key (Frantz and Ezrow, 2011). While revolutions still remain rare, coups and elite dismissals are the most common pathway by which incumbent autocratic leaders are ousted from power (Geddes, 1999, 2005). Elite-based theories argue that, in particular, it is important that a split takes place between hardliners and soft-liners in the regime, which gives the opposition an opening to take advantage of (Przeworski, 1991). On this point, non-violent protests are a particularly important type of resistance, because they increase the likelihood of authoritarian breakdown (Brancati, 2016). One of the reasons why this is the case is because non-violent protests can cause ruptures among the elites. Protests can signal to disaffected elites that they have an opportunity to improve their status by supporting regime breakdown (Haggard and Kaufman, 2016). Elites may believe that they are better off supporting the ousting of an incumbent than face a violent overthrow (Debs, 2016). Regime insiders may also oppose a dictator, but don't know how much support they have. Protests provide these insiders with information of how much discontent there is.

Some studies have also argued that the type of authoritarian regime – or which elites hold power – is important to the outcome (Geddes, 2003; Ulfelder, 2005). Personalist regimes can see contentious collective action pose no significant effect on the risk of regime breakdown. Single-party regimes and military regimes, in contrast, are more likely to break down after non-violent anti-government protests, although military regimes are less likely to break down in the face of riots (Ulfelder, 2005). Personalist regimes have less of a social contract with their citizens than military and single-party regimes, and are unconcerned about the optics of responding with force. The small elite group that surrounds the personalist dictator will be less likely to take on the risk to side with protesters, as there is usually an absence of any other power centres that could challenge the regime. In contrast, in single-party and military regimes, attaining some level of public legitimacy is important. Thus, in the face of non-violent protests, elites may become divided about how to respond.

Protests are also more likely to force the incumbent to exact concessions if the regime perceives itself as weak, and is perceived by the public as weak (Ginkel and Smith, 1999). These concessions may further encourage the protesters to continue to apply pressure to force out even more concessions (Lachapelle and Hellmeier, 2022). Some of the factors that matter in terms of how 'weak' a regime is include how legitimate the regime is perceived by the public, the state of the economy, and how cohesive and loyal the political and military elites are to the regime. But what other factors may signal weakness?

The age of the leader may provide some insight into whether or not protests may be successful in forcing a leader out or exacting concessions, but the leader needs to be well past retirement age of 65 years. Studies have shown that older leaders are more likely to hold competitive elections to reduce uncertainty as the risk of being (violently) ousted by regime insiders or the public may rise the older the dictator is (Tanaka, 2018). An older leader would be more willing to accept a power-sharing arrangement to deal with credible threats from younger and healthier challengers in the regime (Helms, 2020). As dictators age, this also negatively affects economic growth rates (Jong-A-Pin and Mierau, 2022), which in turn could create unrest. But old dictators don't usually lead to democracy, particularly if they die in office. In a study of 79 dictators who died in office from 1946 to 2014, in 92 per cent of these cases, the regime persists after their death, thus remaining autocratic (Kendall-Taylor and Frantz, 2015).

The age of the leader may have mattered in the case of the Arab Spring, but it is more likely other factors were at play. Protests led to Egypt's President Hosni Mubarak stepping down (aged 82 at the time), but Syria's (under Bashir al-Assad – aged 45 at the time) and Libya's (under Muammar Qaddafi – aged 68 at the time) leaders both clung on to power. All of these countries had similar reasons for citizens to be aggrieved, but the outcomes have been very different. Returning to the argument about the importance of elites, some authors argue that successful resistance in authoritarian regimes depends heavily on the security institutions (Chenoweth et al., 2011; Sutton et al., 2014) and, more specifically, how professionalised they are (i.e., are they well paid, well trained, properly equipped, recruited, promoted and demoted based on merit, and trained to respect the civilian authority and population?) (Ezrow and Frantz, 2013). The security institutions include the military, police, secret police and intelligence agencies, and also unofficial actors such as paramilitaries, presidential guards and sometimes death squads (Ezrow, 2017).

The military is traditionally used to defend the country from external threats, but other security institutions are often used to address internal threats to the incumbent regime. If the security institutions that are tasked with protecting the regime are willing to use as much force is necessary against a resisting public, this makes it much more difficult for a dictator to be ousted, even in the face of mass protests. More professionalised security institutions may not want to repress, as they are worried about international prosecution or public retribution. Being asked to repress their own citizens could lead to defectors in the security institutions (Brownlee et al., 2015). It also depends on which part of the security institutions is tasked with doing the regime's dirty work, and how professionalised the military is (Ezrow and Frantz, 2013). Generally, even if it is the police who are responsible for carrying out repression, the military could step in and stage a coup or force the leader to resign.

Thus, the military has important choices to make – it can either respond to protests with repression, which happens about half the time; it can shift its loyalty to the opposition by refusing to use force on its own citizens (referred to as the 'soft defection'), which has happened 37 per cent of the time; or it can decide to stage a coup to oust the leader (referred to as the 'hard defection'), which has happened 15 per cent of the time (Croissant et al., 2018). In the case of Romania, during the wave of revolutions to end communist rule in Europe, the military eventually opted for a soft defection. Protests that erupted in Romania on the 16th of December 1989, starting in Timisoara, a major city in western Romania, were initially met with police repression (Scurtu, 2010). As the protests swelled and were too large for the police to control, the military was sent in, violently clashing with protesters, and, by some reports, over 1,000 people died (Mayr, 2009).

The military was initially loyal to dictator Nicolae Ceauşescu, but was growing tired of being neglected and alienated by the regime, while seeing its responsibility for national defence shared with the Patriotic Guards (Bacon, 2019). As the protests multiplied, Ceauşescu ordered the military to send in tanks, but there was some hesitation from the military. When the Minister of Defence, Vasile Milea, died mysteriously on the 22nd of December after refusing to follow Ceauşescu's orders to step up the violence against civilian protesters, his replacement, Victor Stănculescu, also secretly ordered the army to hold its fire and go back to their barracks (Watts, 2019). Without the military's support, the Ceauşescus were forced to flee and were subsequently tried and executed by firing squad on 25 December 1989.

In the case of Syria, because the security institutions were mostly loyal to the regime and willing to do whatever it took to maintain the status quo, the protests ended by spiralling into conflict. This can partly be explained by the composition of the Syrian military. The upper echelons of the Syrian security forces were filled with Alawites, who are part of the same religious sect as President Bashar al-Assad and his family. Although only 15 per cent of Syrians are Alawite, they account for 90 per cent of those carrying the rank of general or higher (Barany, 2011; Zisser, 2001). Thus, the military was by design moulded to be more loyal to the co-sectarian interests of the regime, rather than to its citizens. Once modest protests started in the city of Deraa in March of 2011, it was the military that was ordered to use excessive force, firing on unarmed protesters and carrying out mass arrests – even bringing in tanks to Deraa by April of that year. Although this triggered significant troop desertions, the military refused to back down even in the face of international condemnation. Syria's praetorian military was much more loyal to Assad than to the innocent civilians (Ezrow and Frantz, 2013).

Libya's military had a similarly personalistic recruitment process. Qaddafi recruited security and intelligence personnel primarily from the Margariha and Werfella clans, and he gave the most responsibility to cronies and family members rather than to individuals with experience. In particular, family members – such as his sons and nephews – were given key positions in the military and he constantly played certain tribes off against one another (Ezrow and Frantz, 2013). Complicating matters, he divided up the military into numerous organisations that had little contact with one another, and he regularly used mercenaries (Black, 2000).

Bahrain also lacks a national military. The military is mostly composed of Sunnis, even though 70 per cent of the country is Shiite. The rest of the security institutions are filled with foreigners who are more likely to be dependent on the regime for their livelihoods than to the Bahraini population. Although the Bahraini military is relatively small and must compete with other security agencies, it is well equipped and well paid. This may explain why Bahrain's Sunni army confirmed its support for the Sunni monarchy of Bahrain by quickly repressing the Shiite revolt (Barany, 2011).

The cases of Egypt and Tunisia also demonstrate how important the role of the military is to resistance efforts. In both Tunisia and Egypt, tribal affiliations are not important (Barany, 2011). Tunisia had a professionalised (and thus not recruited along tribal, ethnic or sectarian lines) but small military that was well trained, while the police, which totalled 130,000 members (or the same number as France) were charged with repressive activities on behalf of the Ben Ali regime. As recently as 2008, the intelligence-based police known as the *mukhabarat* had handily repressed popular protests that broke out in the mining regions in the south-west (Schraeder and Redissi, 2011). However, with the outbreak of more extensive protests in late 2010, the Tunisian military quickly sided with the protesters. Essentially, it boiled down to senior Tunisian military officers not wanting to turn their weapons on the Tunisian people. Many of the Tunisian military troops climbed out of their armoured vehicles and took pictures with protesting citizens. After 28 days of protests that the police were unable to resolve, the military felt it had no choice but to oust Ben Ali.

Egypt's former President Mubarak faced a similar fate at the hands of the military. Egypt's military is one of the most powerful militaries in the developing world, with control over manufacturing and other important industries. Over time, it had been professionalised to mostly focus on the external defence of the nation (Hashim, 2011). Like Tunisia, it also was the police who were responsible for human rights abuses against the public, and it was the military that would eventually come to the rescue. Protests started in Egypt on 25 January 2011 to coincide with the annual police holiday. After clashes with the security institutions killed almost 900 people and injured thousands, by 11 February the military had announced that Mubarak had resigned and should head for internal exile (Schraeder and Redissi, 2011). Although the military had initially hesitated to support the protesters, the generals concluded that Mubarak's regime had crossed the proverbial Rubicon. The regime had engaged in too much repression (most notably, the attacks on civilians on 2 February), and its concessions had failed (such as not allowing his son Gamal to succeed him or seek re-election himself). If the military had continued to back Mubarak, the death toll would have only increased, which in turn would have undermined the military's legitimacy (Barany, 2011).

The security institutions in Iran have thus far remained loyal and united to the interests of the regime. Although there are rumours that there is some reluctance among some of the security and police forces to execute the orders that are given from above, the security forces, including the Islamic Revolutionary Guard Corps, the Basij (a violent volunteer paramilitary militia), the regular army, the police and the intelligence apparatus, all remain committed to preventing any change to the status quo (Safaei, 2023).

Do protests ever lead to real reform?

Generating authoritarian breakdown is significant, but most authoritarian regimes that have been toppled have relapsed into authoritarianism not much longer after the regime was ousted (Geddes et al., 2014). Given that this is the case, it is important to explore when protests might actually lead to real reform. Similar to the logic of authoritarian breakdown, research has shown that when protests involve women, they are more likely to lead to democratic reform and, in some cases, liberal democracy (Chenoweth and Marks, 2022). Women have been important catalysts for pro-democracy movements in Latin America, Southeast Asia and Eastern Europe during the Third Wave. In general, the more inclusive the protest movement is, the more sustainable the negotiated settlement is, and the more durable democracy is likely to be.

Again, non-violence is also important. Once the regime has been toppled, it is non-violent movements that are more likely to promote power sharing and compromise, which are necessary to democracy (Brancati, 2016). In addition to the role of women in ensuring that movements remain non-violent, there is also robust evidence that protest movements with a high degree of involvement by students and well-educated individuals are less likely to turn violent (Dahlum, 2019).

There are several reasons why violent movements fail to lead to real democratic reform. Violent movements are hierarchically organised, will try to eliminate rivals after capturing power, with leaders only including those that fought against the former regime (ibid.). Violent revolutions also tend to bring leaders into power who are particularly aggressive against other states (Colgan and Weeks, 2015) and their own citizens (Kim, 2018). Once the movement becomes violent, the military is more likely to step in and then overthrow the regime and hold on to power (Aksoy et al., 2015). Although the military is often critical to ousting non-democratic leaders, civilian politicians are needed to make real democratic reforms (Slater and Wong, 2013).

In the case of the Philippines, many of the activists who were involved in non-violent political movements of the People Power Revolution were later convinced to run in political campaigns. Their experience participating in a non-violent resistance campaign trained them well to engage in democratic practices. These politicians did not rely on the traditional methods of bribery and intimidation; instead, they employed strategies to appeal to the public good.

Nevertheless, these success stories are more the exception than the norm. Although there are instances where protests can lead to the ousting of a dictator, most protests do not lead to any permanent and meaningful reform. In a study looking at protests from 1946 to 2012, approximately 7 per cent of protests led to the government being ousted, with less than 25 per cent of protests extracting concessions from the government (Kendall-Taylor and Frantz, 2014). Instead, in about two-thirds of protests, the military and police responded with repression, and neighbouring countries took note and cracked down on potential protests as well (ibid.).

In Hong Kong, protesters took to the streets to protest the increasingly repressive environment they faced under Hong Kong's leadership that Beijing presumably controls. The spark in this case was the government's decision in June 2019 to allow extraditions from Hong Kong to China. An estimated one million people took to the streets in response on the 9th of June. Protesters demanded that Hong Kong not only withdraw from the extradition bill, but also release protesters who had been arrested, establish an independent enquiry to investigate police behaviour, and allow for universal suffrage for the Legislative Council elections and the chief executive elections. The movement also demanded that Hong Kong's Chief Executive, Carrie Lam, resign. While young people have been at the forefront of these protests, trade unions, doctors and nurses came out to protest as well.

However, China responded with more force and tightened its grip over Hong Kong. The government cracked down on protesters and instead of conceding to any of the demands, it imposed the Hong Kong National Security Law on the 30th of June 2020. This law criminalises dissent and uses a broad definition of terrorism and collusion with foreign powers to allow Beijing to establish more control over Hong Kong's citizens. Media freedoms were also curbed and the public education system was overhauled to include a curriculum that offers patriotic education. The electoral system was also overhauled in 2021 to ensure that only patriots rule Hong Kong. At one protest on the 16th of June 2019, at least 2 million people, from Hong Kong's population of 7 million, came out, effectively grinding the country to a halt, and yet that was not enough to force any concessions from the government.

The other issue – which remains the case in both Algeria and Sudan – is that although protests may be successful in forcing dictators from power with the military's consent, the military may decide never to actually cede power to civilians. Like their civilian counterparts, military elites have learned how to remain in power after the chaos of a revolution by using clever strategies to weaken and co-opt the civilian opposition. In Sudan, after an optimistic start, the military has shown no signs of relinquishing power and the civilian opposition remains divided about their vision for the future. The cornerstone of Sudan's protest movements was the Sudanese Professionals Association (SPA), an umbrella of labour unions formed by doctors, lawyers and journalists in response to the deteriorating economic conditions, which formed in 2016 (Grewal, 2021). While this movement was effective in organising protests that would lead to Bashir leaving power, since his ousting different civilian groups have made temporary alliances with the military at various times to try to resolve the political dispute, but to no avail. Additionally, under the leadership of Lieutenant-General Abdelfattah al-Burhan (who was appointed after Bashir was ousted), Sudan's military was able to engineer changes to the provisional constitution and eliminated civilian influence over appointments to the new Sovereignty Council and the Cabinet. Thus, when al-Burhan publicly announced that the military would withdraw from politics in July 2022, observers were quick to point out that this was likely a ruse (Ali et al., 2022). Since the announcement, anti-military protests have persisted and the military has done little to cede power to civilians. Constant pressure from civilians on the military will be important if Sudan is to get back on track (Lachapelle and Hellmeier, 2022).

In Algeria, the situation is not that different. While the protest movement in Algeria suffered from less organisation and structure than in Sudan, it was able to convince elites that Bouteflika needed to step down. This wasn't too onerous a task. After Bouteflika's offer not to run for a fifth term did little to quell the protesters, and with Bouteflika suffering from a debilitating stroke in 2013, there was little need for the military to continue to back him. However, Algeria has seen only a change in who the president is; the military regime never really left.

The military in Algeria has remained fairly united with General Gaid Salah taking over after Bouteflika was ousted and limiting potential internal challenges by arresting the head of the intelligence services, the Département du renseignement et de la sécurité (DRS), and his successor. The military has also engaged in a combination of divide-and-rule tactics along ethnic lines to stifle the opposition, such as arresting protesters waving the Amazigh flag, the flag of the Berber population, which constitutes 23 per cent of the population. Prominent opposition figures have been arrested, as have hundreds of other protesters. Meanwhile, other opposition members have been co-opted – releasing 10,000 political prisoners, but keeping others in prison. New Algerian President, Abdelmadjid Tebboune, dissolved parliament in February 2021 and tried to hold new elections that saw very low turnout (23 per cent). Like most authoritarian regimes described in earlier chapters, Algeria is an electoral authoritarian regime – elections take place, but there is no democratic rule or representation (see Chapter 2). The Algerian opposition has also been unable to rally around a unified roadmap due to the lack of a leader for its Hirak Movement. Although Hirak shows little sign of disbanding, without a leader it faces an uphill battle to push for real reforms that have lasting power.

Challenges and opportunities for new protest movements

The opportunities that new protest movements face also serve as potential challenges. For example, the lack of leadership is a relatively new phenomenon. Most of the protests that took place in the post-Cold War period (1989–2011) were organised by political parties and their supporters two-thirds of the time (Brancati, 2016). However, in the recent protest cycles, we see that there is no clear leader to help frame and shape the movement, which is critical to a movement's success. Leaders can articulate messages in ways that attract a wider constituency and draw people in. Leaders are also able to maintain unity, prevent schisms and prevent factions from engaging in risky behaviour that would be ineffective to the cause.

Protest groups that are disorganised are more likely to become involved in violence because there is less discipline, no clear hierarchy and objectives (Ives and Lewis, 2020). Movements with more centralised information structures are also better able to process the intelligence they receive and coordinate a clear and persistent strategy.

In addition to being leaderless, the most recent protest cycles have seen little cooperation between protesters with political parties and the mainstream media. Protests are most likely to succeed if they have organisational capacity (Sutton et al., 2014). Thus, although protests are often grievance-driven, protests are more likely to happen when there are political opportunities (known as 'opportunity-based approaches' to social movements), such as when activists have organisational capacity. This can come in the form of mobilising structures such as political organisations and networks. Protesters are more likely to protest when they are active in one or more civic or political organisation (Thyen and Gerschewski, 2018).

Instead, protesters relied on the internet and public places for collective debate. The Hong Kong protests have essentially been leaderless and have drawn inspiration from martial arts star Bruce Lee to make the movement 'like water', as water is shapeless and formless, and therefore more difficult to control (Holbig, 2020: 331). And while the Hong Kong movement lacked a clear structure, activists coordinated using secure apps such as Telegram and other apps to identify and avoid police deployments. That brings us to the question of what role technology has had in facilitating protests.

Studies have shown that increasing internet use boosts the likelihood of protests in authoritarian regimes, and social media has facilitated protests in a number of ways (Enikolopov et al., 2020; Jost et al., 2018; Tudoroiu, 2014). In authoritarian regimes, the major mass-communication channels were controlled by authoritarian regimes like newspapers, radio and television, but the internet allows for real communication without centralised control. Social media has allowed users to communicate their grievances more rapidly and to a much wider audience. The internet allows people to absorb information that is different from the government. Citizens are more likely to be exposed to government failures, civic debates and alternative ideas. This can help produce attitudinal change. Social media also helps activists overcome collective action problems, communicating quickly with a wide audience, where protests will take place and how many people might attend, which decreases the informational uncertainty. The internet helps to address the risks associated with protesting by providing certainty that others are also going to take to the street. The internet also helps protesters communicate to others about the severity, location and type of state repression, reducing the costs and risks for those members of the opposition. With social media, the costs of communicating about protest decreases as well, as they are no longer hampered by spatial and temporal barriers, such as the need to physically hand out flyers, make phone calls or send individual texts. People can find out about protests in real time and decide to join them spontaneously. As social media users are not journalists, they can disseminate information in more emotional, personal, provocative and motivational ways since they are not bound by professional norms of objectivity. Social media may also help mobilise potential protesters by spreading dramatic images and videos, as was the case during the Arab Spring and the 2022 protests in Iran. One study showed using data from 1990 to 2013 that internet usage increased the expected number of protests in authoritarian regimes but not democracies (Ruijgrok, 2017).

The issue is that social media may help protesters coordinate and bring out protesters en masse, but it does not guarantee that autocratic breakdown or democracy will follow. Social media is not helpful in fostering strong ties needed to form civil society groups that work collectively together in person (Cabrera et al., 2017). Activism is hard work, and toppling authoritarian rule often takes years of persistent resistance involving a wide array of actors, including human rights groups and networks, civil society groups, labour movements and even church groups which are critical to authoritarian breakdown (Brancati, 2016). For this reason, protests that have a clear organisational structure and leadership are more likely to be successful.

When talking about social media, it is important to return to the case of Iran's 2022 protests. The protests captured the world's attention due to the vivid imagery, which had largely been driven by women. Some of the notable images captured headscarves being burned, and women cutting their hair and dancing in defiance. Strikes were reported in schools, universities and the country's vital oil sector, while shops repeatedly shut their doors. At the World Cup in November, Iran's football team refused to sing their national anthem and fans have chanted slogans against the regime, such as 'women, life, freedom', a phrase connected to the Kurdish liberation struggle. Some media outlets reported that these were one of the largest and most prolonged protests in recent history, uniting nearly every section of society, pushing for regime change.

The problem is that in spite of the striking imagery of protesters taking to the streets, the movement is leaderless and lacks organisation, which will make it easier for the regime to contain it. Most of the protests have taken place spontaneously and have been organised through Instagram and TikTok. Although the lack of a leader means that it is harder to decapitate the movement (by taking out its leader), this also means that it would lack organisational capacity, which would make it easier for the state to overpower the protesters.

In comparison, Iran's Green Movement in 2009 (driven by fraudulent elections) was better organised, drawing from a vast organisational network that was built up after months of intensive campaigning in the presidential elections. The Green Movement had a headquarters, which involved political parties, student and labour organisations, and was led by new opposition leaders like Mousavi and Karroubi who had a long history of working within the regime. The press erroneously labelled the movement the 'Twitter Revolution', but demonstrations were actually organised through careful planning, word of mouth, mobile phone calls and texts. Although the Green Movement was able to draw millions to the streets, only a small amount of effort was needed to contain the demonstrations in a matter of months (Safaei, 2023).

The Green Movement may have also had more knowledgeable protesters who had some sense of political efficacy due to their experience working in politics. In contrast to research that largely focuses on grievances and opportunities, studies that focus on cognitive politicisation look at the cognitive abilities and political trust levels of the protesters themselves. Accordingly, this research suggests that grievances are most likely to spark protest movements, when protesters have a high sense of political efficacy and low levels of political trust (Van Stekelenburg and Klandermans, 2013). This may explain why so many protesters are students. They are not only well educated, but they remain energetic and optimistic about the possibility of forcing meaningful change (Brancati, 2016).

The dictator dilemma of how to respond to protests

Responding to protesters presents a major dilemma for dictators. Protests are not just destabilising; they impose significant political and economic costs for incumbent authoritarian regimes (Ulfelder, 2005), with even non-violent protests associated with a 1.7 per cent decline in economic growth (Lachapelle and Hellmeier, 2022). Most studies have argued that when faced with violent forms of protest activity that may become more widespread, states are likely to respond with repression (Boudreau, 2002; Regan and Henderson, 2002). Repression is actually less costly in this instance versus accommodation (Pierskalla, 2010), as concessions and the reduction of state repression may be seen as a political opportunity in authoritarian regimes, making contentious politics less risky for protesters.

However, how a regime responds to peaceful protests presents more of a dilemma. Authoritarian regimes may first want to engage in co-optation of some protesters by accommodating some of their demands or distributing some economic and political benefits (Sanches, 2022). Additionally, authoritarian regimes might respond with violence if accommodation has not worked in the past (Moore, 2000). Nevertheless, if the regime responds with repression, this may encourage further mobilisation against the regime (Chenoweth et al., 2011), or more commonly may lead to international condemnation and sanctions (Levitsky and Way, 2010). Some scholars counter that repression is usually successful for authoritarian regimes because it makes it more difficult for protest movements to recruit and motivate participants (Davenport, 2015). Repression can demoralise the opposition and demobilise them, particularly when repression is applied against protests that are not part of a broader ongoing campaign of non-violent resistance (Sutton et al., 2014).

However, others counter that repression may only work to reduce dissent in the short term, but will increase dissident activity in the long run (Francisco, 2004; Heath et al., 2000). Mobilisation rebounds after state repression as anger grows over government abuse (Kurtz and Smithey, 2018). People may be more likely take to the streets when repression increases, particularly if demands are not being addressed (Osa and Schock, 2007). It is also noted that repression of non-violent activity may actually backfire and reduce non-violent protests but increase the chances of violent strategies being used (Ezrow, 2017; Lichbach, 1987). One study that looked at over 6,000 incidents of non-violent protest across Africa from 2000 to 2015, found that protests are most likely to escalate into violence if repression has been used recently (Ives and Lewis, 2020). Exposure to different types of repression (such as torture and arrests) also helps to upskill a resistance movement that helps the movement later on (Finkel et al., 2015). Because repression can lead to significant political backlash, sophisticated surveillance apparatuses are increasingly used to monitor behaviour and detect movements towards overt collective challenges before they become too powerful and effective (Sullivan, 2016).

The objective of the protest may also matter. Protests that erupt that aim for regime change or some other substantial change to the socio-economic order may face much more repression than protests that take place targeting local governments, localised issues or specific institutions that are distinct from the incumbent regime. In the Arab Spring, while the republics were rocked by regime ending protests, many of the monarchies faced protests that posed little threat to their rule. In Jordan and Morocco, protesters were not objecting to the monarchy per se, but were dissatisfied with the political institutions that were failing to address corruption and under-representation (Barari and Satkowski, 2012). Rather than respond with force, the police in Jordan were spotted shaking hands with protesters and handing out juice and bottled water (Amos, 2013).

China offers another example. China is one of the most repressive regimes in the world, where one could argue that there should be few opportunities for protests to take place, but one study noted that over 5,300 protests took place from 2000 to 2013 (Chen, 2017). Even more surprising is that most of the information on these protests was broadcast by the official Chinese media (Huang et al., 2019). For example, state-controlled national media outlets provided in-depth coverage of unprecedented taxi drivers' strikes that took place in Chongqing in November 2008, when 9,000 drivers stopped working in protest against fuel shortages and management fees. The media coverage was so thorough that it led to strikes in 18 other cities making similar demands. While this may seem counter-intuitive that the government would allow the grievances to be nationally broadcast, these protests posed little threat to the stability of the regime. The strikes only targeted local officials and local corruption. Allowing the media to diffuse this information helps the regime to identify local grievances before they fester and grow into national-level resentment. It also forces local governments to do better in addressing local citizen grievances (Huang et al., 2019).

In spite of the tempered response to protests that target local grievances, most national protests are met with force. In fact, nearly 90 per cent of the 108 non-violent campaigns experienced violent repression by the state (Chenoweth et al., 2011). For example, in Rwanda and Ethiopia, protests have been met with repression (Mueller, 2020). And the same could be said about Zimbabwe, as former president Mugabe was willing to use violence against both violent revolutionaries and non-violent protesters (Ives and Lewis, 2020).

The case of Iran illustrates the steps the state is willing to go to defend the status quo. Since the 2019 protests over fuel price hikes, the regime has completely excluded moderates from participating at all. The Guardian Council, the unelected 12-body member body that vets the candidates, has prevented moderate candidates from running and only allowed hardliner candidates to run. Even moderate conservatives like former Speaker of the Parliament, Ali Larijani, have been banned from running. Electoral fraud and voter apathy are so rampant that there were more invalid votes recorded (3.84 million) than votes for the runner-up candidate, Mohsen Rezaee (3.44 million) (Safaei, 2023).

In looking again at Iran's 2022 protests, we can see that the Iranian security apparatus had few qualms about violently squashing them. Well over 500 people were killed and more than 20,000 people were detained, including journalists, lawyers and celebrities. Some protesters have faced torture while in detention, while a select few have already been sentenced to death. Alarmingly, weapons that are usually used in war zones have been fired on protesters indiscriminately. And, just like the numerous protests beforehand, the protests that started in 2022 are not likely to be met with any reforms. It is more likely that we will witness even more repression and greater levels of militarisation than any attempt to address the concerns of protesters.

Conclusion

Although much has been uncovered about how authoritarian regimes function and maintain themselves in power, less is known about how much agency domestic actors have in expediting authoritarian breakdown and encouraging meaningful reforms. There have been many studies on these topics, but no magic formula. For the most part, the literature has been pessimistic about how successful domestic resistance will be in their objectives. Protests often make international headlines, arouse people to take to the streets, but are usually met with excessive force and little accommodation. Although protests are often seen as a crack in the armour of authoritarian regimes, most democratic protest movements do not meet their objectives, and protesters are often arrested, imprisoned and/or killed.

However, state violence does not render people helpless. As the chapter has laid out, protests are more likely to be successful when they are part of a protest cycle; when they are inclusive and non-violent, and involve women; and when they can capitalise on elite splits, particularly in the security institutions. Protests also create dilemmas for authoritarian regimes – they push autocrats to use repressive tactics when they may not want to.

Although most authoritarian regimes are using less force than in the past, there are a growing number of authoritarian regimes that have become more brazen and aggressive with other countries, more cooperative with one another and more involved in the economies and political affairs of other regimes around the world. It is not just that China has been exerting itself more forcefully in the South China Sea; that Russia pursued airstrikes in Syria in 2015 and invaded Ukraine in 2014 and again in 2022; that Iran has upped its activity in Afghanistan, Iraq, Yemen and Lebanon; that Saudi Arabia has engaged in a long bombing campaign in Yemen. Authoritarian regimes have been more willing to use their military power – signs of a changing international environment. The concluding chapter will explore these issues more in depth.

conclusion

- New authoritarian threat.
- Summary of the key points.

The New Authoritarian Threat

The world doesn't seem to be in a very good place right now. We started this book by looking at the Russian invasion of Ukraine. Indeed, in addition to the changing nature of authoritarian regimes, autocracies have also transformed their foreign policies and strategies, and some have become more aggressive. This contrasts with just after the Cold War ended, when authoritarian regimes were focused on their own survival. Several decades later, this is no longer the case, as autocratic regimes – namely, China and Russia – are trying to increase their spheres of influence, supporting authoritarianism outside their borders and even working to undermine democracy in some instances. Let's go into further detail about the new authoritarian threat – namely, how authoritarian regimes are aggressively spreading authoritarian norms and values, something that is sometimes referred to as 'autocratic promotion' or 'autocratic diffusion'. We will first look at how authoritarian regimes are collaborating and learning from one another.

Authoritarian collaboration and learning – team authoritarian?

Are authoritarian regimes loyal to one another? Not necessarily, but they are willing to work together, particularly if it comes at the expense of democracies. In the Cold War, you had the West supporting and working with right-wing dictatorships in efforts to combat left-wing authoritarianism. Today, you have the likes of Russia under Putin, which is borderline fascist, being chummy with left-wing Venezuelan leaders like Maduro and Chávez. Maduro even went as far as to award Putin with Venezuela's first annual peace prize in 2016!

Giving each other inane prizes is just the start of it. Authoritarian collaboration and learning are notable trends that have facilitated the durability of authoritarian forms of rule. With authoritarian learning, autocracies observe other autocracies to learn about how to repress and adjust their tactics from information they have gained by watching others – both from their successes and failures. China has learned from the chaotic dissolution of the Soviet Union. Iran has learned from Syria's methods of dealing with mass demonstrations (Olar, 2019).

Authoritarian regimes are also sharing key strategies to help sustain themselves in power, such as how to hold elections without sparking the ire of international observers (Von Soest, 2015). Shared training exercises are also held to help countries deal with organised dissent. Russia held a conference in Moscow on International Security in May 2014 to help other authoritarian regimes deal more effectively with protests. States like Hungary have learned from Russia and have implemented deceptive laws in order to muzzle and stifle foreign NGOs and the free media (Ambrosio, 2020).

China has also offered training programmes and seminars on information management and monitoring systems, and has held conferences to learn how to censor and monitor negative opinions, and to learn about its cybersecurity laws which brought in representatives from Egypt, Jordan, Lebanon, Libya, Morocco, Saudi Arabia and the United Arab Emirates. Yes, believe it or not, there is training offered on how to be a better dictatorship. Other countries have been inspired by China and have passed similar laws after receiving bilateral training. A training session of Vietnamese officials in April 2017 led to the introduction of new cybersecurity laws that matched those in China in 2018. Uganda and Tanzania also introduced Chinese-inspired cybersecurity laws in their countries as well (Shahbaz, 2018). Inspired by or learning from China, over the last two decades internet shutdowns, online surveillance, social media taxes and imprisonment over anti-government posts have taken place in countries such as Chad, Ethiopia, Zimbabwe, the Republic of Congo, Burundi, Togo, Guinea, Tanzania and Uganda. China has created a network of media elites and government ministers around the world that are following suit on its internet policy. Countries that regularly interact with one another may end up emulating the practices and values of the more powerful partner in areas such as business, administration and politics (Lankina et al., 2016).

Authoritarian regimes have also become more cooperative with one another, leading to an increase in authoritarian practices around the world. By collaboration, we are referring to instances where regimes are providing each other with various forms of support to help maintain authoritarian rule. Russia has offered low-cost digital disinformation tools to help other illiberal states repress their own populations, while China is the number one supplier of surveillance and monitoring systems. Senegal, for example, has used Chinese equipment and technical support to improve its surveillance technology (Lamensch, 2021). In Sub-Saharan Africa, at least 24 countries use Chinese surveillance technology (ibid.). Venezuela has contracted Chinese technology to build their own database to track individuals' transactions. Surveillance technology has been sold to Ecuador, and facial recognition technology has been sold to the United Arab Emirates. As China has a close relationship with Chinese tech companies such as Huawei, their technicians have helped the regimes in Uganda and Zambia to spy on their political opponents (Bagwandeen, 2021).

Beijing has also promoted the Digital Silk Road (DSR), which encompasses the fibre-optic cables, mobile networks, satellite relay stations, data centres and smart cities built by global Chinese technology companies. Through these investments, the Chinese government aims to exert political influence around the world, particularly in Asia, Africa and Latin America. Africa has been a particular focus of Chinese investment, with over 350 Chinese technological initiatives. Additionally, the arrival of Chinese engineers, managers and diplomats expose these countries to the Chinese models for governing the internet (Qiang, 2021).

China has already collaborated with countries such as Pakistan, Thailand, Ethiopia, Nigeria, Laos, Sri Lanka, Sudan and Turkey (Qiang, 2021). Myanmar, Vietnam, Sri Lanka, Laos, Malaysia, Cambodia and Singapore also all cooperate with China in terms of procurement and the preparation of digital policies such as creating smart cities, facial recognition technology and smart policing (Wijayanto et al., 2022). China and Russia have also directly collaborated on a joint investment project to share big data and use artificial intelligence to facilitate cross-border commercial activities (Sinkkonen and Lassila, 2022).

Soft and Sharp Power

The major authoritarian regimes also want to influence politics beyond their own borders. More and more, they do this through using soft power and sharp power. Soft power is the ability to shape the preferences of other states through persuasion and attraction. Countries like China, Russia, Turkey and Saudi Arabia are flexing their soft power by setting up intercultural people-to-people exchanges, educational institutes, media enterprises such as international news networks, and numerous investments in real estate and infrastructure (Ambrosio, 2010; Hall and Ambrosio, 2017; Kneuer and Demmelhuber, 2016; Roberts and Ziemer, 2018; Ziegler, 2016). China and Russia have spent billions to shape public opinion and perceptions around the world, with China likely spending about $10 billion a year (Shambaugh, 2015). These actions are intended to shape perspectives, gain a wider audience and incentivise cooperation. There has been a growth of propaganda networks by Russia as well, such as the Russkiy Mir Foundation and Rosstrudnichestvo, which supposedly promote education and culture, the Russian language and the Russian

World (Lankina and Niemczyk, 2015). China and Russia also shape narratives abroad through their state-owned international media organisations (CCTV and Russia Today, respectively), which have a growing presence in the US, Africa, the Middle East and Latin America (Walker, 2016).

China has also grown increasingly assertive and confident that its political–economic model is more capable of weathering various crises (Zhao, 2010). As part of the aforementioned China's Digital Silk Road, more states are interacting with Beijing in order to access loans without conditions, trade and financial aid. This all impacts the appeal of China's model vis-à-vis a democratic one (Ambrosio, 2012).

In addition to using soft power to spread authoritarian norms and to tout their successes, they are using sharp power to surreptitiously undercut democracies. Sharp power is how a regime chips away at their enemies without having to use force. More formally, sharp power is the ability to perforate, pierce and penetrate political environments by manipulating information and creating distractions (Cardenal and Cerulli, 2018; Walker, 2018). The classic example is Russian interference in democratic elections in the US, France, the UK, Ukraine and Georgia (this type of sharp power will be discussed in more detail in the next section). Sharp power camouflages state-directed projects to look as though they are the works of commercial media or a grassroots organisation. These projects are tools of propaganda or foreign manipulation, not just to neutralise criticism, but to support authoritarianism and authoritarian elements in vulnerable democracies.

The use of technology to manipulate a foreign population has reshaped the power balance between democracies and autocracies (Kendall-Taylor et al., 2019). The Kremlin has spread negative narratives about the European Union (EU) to shape the opinion of Russian speakers in European countries. The EU is depicted as aggressive on one hand, but also too weak and amoral to deal with global challenges (Dimitrova et al., 2017). The Russian government has also developed cooperative agreements with political parties in Europe that represent Russian minorities in countries like Estonia, Ukraine, Moldovia and Latvia to further undercut democracy there (Dimitrova et al., 2017).

As already mentioned, authoritarian regimes use technology to flood social media with false or confusing information that is designed to create confusion in their own countries. But some authoritarian regimes are also using these same tactics to stoke polarisation abroad as well, and to support authoritarian forces in democracies. One of the most common tactics of authoritarian regimes is to flood social media with fake news, particularly before elections in vulnerable democracies, as was the case with Russia's electoral interference in the 2016 US presidential election. In France and Germany in 2017, Russian government operatives used a disinformation campaign to help promote far-right groups supportive of Russia's agenda, including the German far-right party, Alternative fur Deutschland (AfD). Russian hackers also targeted Emmanuel Macron's presidential campaign in France, leaking the contents of his campaign's email server in the final days of the campaign. Sometimes the use of bots is used to wedge a divide between authoritarian regimes and democratic states. Russian bots launched a campaign that Turkey should file an international lawsuit against US President Joe Biden, due to his recognition of the Armenian genocide. Another Russian campaign indicated that Biden was the reason for the CAATSA sanctions against Turkey, and not Trump, even though the sanctions were issued under the Trump administration (Qiang, 2021).

Iranian government hackers have also targeted the US and other Western European democracies (Michaelsen, 2018). Not to be outdone, the worst offenders in disseminating false information abroad (and domestically) are Turkmenistan, Venezuela, Syria, Myanmar and Eritrea (Mechkova et al., 2022).

These regimes have identified ways to compromise the values of transparency and accountability and to export corruption to democracies. For example, under Vladimir Putin, a centrepiece of Russia's engagement with the West has been the corrupt and exploitative export of hydrocarbons, which has had an impact on Western financial, legal and political institutions. While elites directly linked with Russia act as gatekeepers to prevent pro-EU linkages, Western universities, think tanks and technological companies have become more integrated with authoritarian systems, enabling these regimes to co-opt their Western partners by shaping norms of free expression.

Key points

This book has laid out the ways in which dictatorships function today, and how these new forms of dictatorship have evolved. The first chapter started by describing the landscape of authoritarianism and noted the trends of autocratisation, and, more specifically, authoritarian deepening and personalisation of politics. The chapter that followed looked at how authoritarian regimes are defined and classified, bringing you up to speed with the various continuous measures of dictatorship, along with other ways of classifying dictatorships into categories based on who holds power, instead of based on degrees of democracy or autocracy.

After setting the foundation for what we mean by autocracy, the next chapter explored all the things we know about authoritarianism today. Building on the information in Chapter 2 on electoral autocracies, the chapter explained how new forms of autocracy have developed that appear to represent a break from the past, and at first glance, seem more democratic, but actually constitute a more resilient version of autocracy rather than a distant relative. This democratic veneer of pseudo-democratic institutions cloaks the true authoritarian nature of the regime. While elections, legislatures, judiciaries, constitutions and fake NGOs provide the façade of democratic governance, technology is harnessed to exert greater levels of control and surveillance over citizens, causing them to be confused, apathetic and disillusioned.

What is still a bit of an unknown is what role the public can play in pushing back against rising levels of authoritarianism, particularly the new form of authoritarianism today. Are protests ever effective in toppling tyrants? Thus far, the answer is most likely not in the short term. However, constant pressure from civil society can eventually reap rewards for democratic forces. Although electoral authoritarian regimes are lasting longer than ever, holding elections provides a sliver of hope for the opposition to break through, or at least may force the incumbent to resort to fraud to 'win', something that can incite the public to protest. These push-and-pull factors make the next decade an interesting time to study authoritarian regimes. History shows that autocratic periods don't last forever.

Most scholars agree that democracies tend to cluster in time and space, something referred to as 'waves of democracy' (Huntington, 1993). As Chapters 1 and 3 explained, the same can also be said of authoritarian regimes. Although not studied as frequently, autocratic diffusion denotes that there are periods of time when autocracies spread, particularly in certain regions. Autocratic values have spread, autocracies have learned from one another, and more and more countries have become autocratic.

Today, there are certain authoritarian power centres that are actively undermining democratic development and cooperating with one another, which has prolonged this current wave of autocratisation. Most scholarly attention has focused on Russia and China, but states like Iran, Saudi Arabia and Venezuela have also had a negative impact in their neighbourhoods and beyond. Russia is undoubtably the most active authoritarian actor in the push to undermine democracy around the world. Its efforts to do so have been substantial and have had a significant impact on human life.

Not surprisingly, there has been a concerted focus on Ukraine in its battle to defend itself against Putin's invasion. Ukrainian President Volodymyr Zelensky has framed Ukraine as the lynchpin in the fight against authoritarianism. Indeed, this is not a huge exaggeration. The fate of many countries whose political development has been impacted negatively by Russia hangs in the balance, such as Georgia, Armenia, Kyrgyzstan and, of course, Ukraine. Other countries that look to Russia include Hungary, Bulgaria and Serbia, and a weaker Russia could affect autocratic forces in these countries as well. As Russia continues to struggle in its quest to control Ukraine, it is draining some of its resources. It is hard to imagine that it will emerge stronger than ever after this prolonged conflict ends, in spite of Putin's oddly high approval rating.

Additionally, waves of autocratisation have been met with serious protest (as Chapter 4 explained). And while most protests are unsuccessful, citizens have been using every means possible to voice their dissatisfaction and frustration. As regimes continue to overreach, citizens are pushing back, coordinating together, and resisting autocratic power grabs that are infringing on their rights and freedoms. Based on historical patterns, the natural ebb and flow of these different waves means that we are due for a new era of autocratic breakdowns in the near future.

references

Aksoy, D., Carter, D.B. and Wright, J. (2015) 'Terrorism and the fate of dictators', *World Politics*, 67 (3): 423–68.

Ali, H., Ben Hammou, S. and Powell, J.M. (2022) 'Between coups and election: constitutional engineering and military entrenchment in Sudan', *Africa Spectrum*, 57 (3): 327–39.

Ambrosio, T. (2010) 'Constructing a framework of authoritarian diffusion: concepts, dynamics, and future research', *International Studies Perspectives*, 11 (4): 375–92.

Ambrosio, T. (2012) 'The rise of the "China Model" and "Beijing Consensus": evidence of authoritarian diffusion?', *Contemporary Politics*, 18 (4): 381–99.

Ambrosio, T. (2020) 'Russia's effects on a consolidated democracy: the erosion of democracy in Hungary and the Putin model', in *Authoritarian Gravity Centers*. London: Routledge. pp. 175–202.

Amnesty International (2022) 'Belarus 2022'. Available at: www.amnesty.org/en/location/europe-and-central-asia/belarus/report-belarus/ (accessed 3 October 2023).

Amos, D. (2013) 'In a rough neighborhood, Jordan clings to its stability', *NPR*, 1 July. Available at: www.npr.org/sections/parallels/2013/07/01/196656296/stability-or-democracy-in-jordan-its-a-fragile-balance (accessed 3 October 2023).

Associated Press (2022) 'Nicaragua cancels nearly 200 NGOs in sweeping purge of civil society', *The Guardian*, 2 June. Available at: www.theguardian.com/world/2022/jun/02/nicaragua-cancels-non-governmental-organizations-civil-society (accessed 3 October 2023).

Ayalew, Y.E. (2021) 'From digital authoritarianism to platforms' leviathan power: freedom of expression in the digital age under siege in Africa', *Mizan Law Review*, 15 (2): 455–92.

Bacon, W.M. (2019) 'Romanian civil–military relations after 1989', in *The Military and Society in the Former Eastern Bloc*. Abingdon: Routledge. pp. 179–200.

Bagwandeen, M. (2021) 'Don't blame China for the rise of digital authoritarianism in Africa', *Africa at LSE*.

Balasubramaniam, R.R. (2009) 'Judicial politics in authoritarian regimes', *University of Toronto Law Journal*, 59 (3): 405–16.

Barari, H.A. and Satkowski, C.A. (2012) 'The Arab spring: the case of Jordan', *Ortadoğu Etütleri*, 3 (2): 41–58.

Barany, Z. (2011) 'Comparing the Arab revolts: the role of the military', *Journal of Democracy*, 22 (4): 24–35.

Baturo, A. and Elkink, J. (2021) *The New Kremlinology: Understanding Regime Personalization in Russia*. Oxford: Oxford University Press.

BBC News (2012) 'Mali's ex-leader Amadou Toumani Toure flees to Senegal', 20 April. Available at: ww.bbc.co.uk/news/world-africa-17782979 (accessed 3 October 2023).

BBC News (2021) 'Nicaragua opposition figure Chamorro put under house arrest', 3 June. Available at: ww.bbc.co.uk/news/world-latin-america-57341542 (accessed 3 October 2023).

Beardsworth, N., Cheeseman, N. and Tinhu, S. (2019) 'Zimbabwe: the coup that never was, and the election that could have been', *African Affairs*, 118 (472): 580–96.

Bermeo, N. (2016) 'On democratic backsliding', *Journal of Democracy*, 27 (1): 5–19.

Bernhard, M.B., Edgell, A. and Lindberg, S.I. (2020) 'Institutionalising electoral uncertainty and authoritarian regime survival', *European Journal of Political Research*, 59 (2): 465–87.

Beswick, D. (2011) 'Aiding state building and sacrificing peace building? The Rwanda–UK relationship 1994–2011', *Third World Quarterly*, 32 (10): 1911–30.

Bhasin, T. and Gandhi, J. (2013) 'Timing and targeting of state repression in authoritarian elections', *Electoral Studies*, 32 (4): 620–31.

Birch, S. (2011). *Electoral Malpractice*. New York: Oxford University Press.

Biswas, S. (2021) 'Why journalists in India are under attack', BBC News, 4 February. Available at: www.bbc.co.uk/news/world-asia-india-55906345 (accessed 3 October 2023).

Black, C.R. (2000) *Deterring Libya: The Strategic Culture of Muammar Qaddafi*. Air University Maxwell Air Force Base AL.

Blaydes, L. (2010) *Elections and Distributive Politics in Mubarak's Egypt*. Cambridge: Cambridge University Press.

Blaydes, L. (2018) *State of Repression: Iraq under Saddam Hussein*. Princeton: Princeton University Press.

Boas, T.C. (2006) 'Weaving the authoritarian web: the control of internet use in nondemocratic regimes' in *How Revolutionary Was the Digital Revolution*? Stanford, CA: Stanford Business Books.

Boix, C. and Svolik, M.W. (2013) 'The foundations of limited authoritarian government: institutions, commitment, and power-sharing in dictatorships', *The Journal of Politics*, 75 (2): 300–16.
Boudreau, V. (2002) 'State repression and democracy protest in three Southeast Asian countries', in D.S. Meyer et al. (eds), *Social Movements: Identity, Culture and the State*. Oxford: Oxford University Press. pp. 28–46.
Brancati, D. (2016) *Democracy Protests*. Cambridge: Cambridge University Press.
Brancati, D. and Lucardi, A. (2019) 'What we (do not) know about the diffusion of democracy protests, *Journal of Conflict Resolution*, 63 (10): 2438–49.
Bratton, M. (2008) 'Vote buying and violence in Nigerian election campaigns', *Electoral Studies*, 27 (4): 621–32.
Bratton, M. and Masunungure, E. (2007) 'Popular reactions to state repression: operation Murambatsvina in Zimbabwe', *African Affairs*, 106 (422): 21–45.
Bratton, M. and Van de Walle, N. (1994) 'Neopatrimonial regimes and political transitions in Africa', *World Politics*, 46 (4): 453–89.
Brownlee, J. (2007) *Authoritarianism in an Age of Democratization.* Cambridge: Cambridge University Press. p. 10.
Brownlee, J., Masoud, T.E., Masoud, T. and Reynolds, A. (2015) *The Arab Spring: Pathways of Repression and Reform*. New York: Oxford University Press.
Bunce, V. (2017) 'The prospects for a color revolution in Russia', *Daedalus*, 146 (2): 19–29.
Bunce, V.J. and Wolchik, S.L. (2006) 'International diffusion and postcommunist electoral revolutions', *Communist and Post-Communist Studies*, 39 (3): 283–304.
Bunce, V.J. and Wolchik, S.L. (2011) *Defeating Authoritarian Leaders in Postcommunist Countries*. Cambridge: Cambridge University Press.
Burkhardt, F. (2020) 'The institutionalization of personalism? The presidency and the president after Putin's constitutional overhaul', *Russian Analytical Digest* (250), pp. 5–10.
Buzogány, A. (2017) 'Illiberal democracy in Hungary: authoritarian diffusion or domestic causation?', *Democratization*, 24 (7): 1307–25.
Byman, D. and Lind, J. (2010) 'Pyongyang's survival strategy: tools of authoritarian control in North Korea', *International Security*, 35 (1): 44–74.
Cabrera, N.L., Matias, C.E. and Montoya, R. (2017) 'Activism or slacktivism? The potential and pitfalls of social media in contemporary student activism', *Journal of Diversity in Higher Education*, 10 (4): 400.
Cañizález, A. (2014) 'The state in pursuit of hegemony over the media: the Chávez model', in M.A. Guerrero and M. Marquez-Ramirez (eds), *Media Systems and Communication Policies in Latin America*. New York: Palgrave Macmillan. pp. 157–77.

Cardenal, J.P. and Cerulli, L.G. (2018) *El «poder incisivo» de China en América Latina y el caso argentino*. CADAL.

Carey, S.C. (2010) 'The use of repression as a response to domestic dissent', *Political Studies*, 58 (1): 167–86.

Carothers, T. (2002) 'The end of the transition paradigm', *Journal of Democracy*, 13 (1): 5–21.

Castillo, H. (2022) 'The worst year for independent media' in Nicaragua. *VOA News*, 26 December. Available at: www.voanews.com/a/the-worst-year-for-independent-media-in-nicaragua/6873829.html (accessed 10 November 2023).

Chehabi, H.E., Linz, J.J. and Chehabi, H.E. (eds) (1998) *Sultanistic Regimes*. Baltimore, MD: Johns Hopkins University Press.

Chen, C.J.J. (2017) 'Policing protest in China: findings from newspaper data', *Taiwanese Sociology*, 33: 113–64.

Chen, W., Zhong, Y. and Zheng, Y. (2005) 'The 16th National Congress of the Chinese Communist Party: institutionalization of succession politics', *Leadership in a Changing China*, pp. 15–36.

Chenoweth, E. (2021) *Civil Resistance: What Everyone Needs to Know*. Oxford: Oxford University Press.

Chenoweth, E. and Belgioioso, M. (2019) 'The physics of dissent and the effects of movement momentum', *Nature Human Behaviour*, 3 (10): 1088–95.

Chenoweth, E. and Marks, Z. (2022) 'Revenge of the patriarchs: why autocrats fear women', *Foreign Affairs*, 101: 103.

Chenoweth, E., Stephan, M.J. and Stephan, M. (2011) *Why Civil Resistance Works: The Strategic Logic of Nonviolent Conflict*. New York: Columbia University Press.

Colgan, J.D. and Weeks, J.L. (2015) 'Revolution, personalist dictatorships, and international conflict', *International Organization*, 69 (1): 163–94.

Collier, D. and Levitsky, S. (1997) 'Democracy with adjectives: conceptual innovation in comparative research', *World Politics*, 49 (3): 430–51.

Cook. E. (2023) 'Putin's popularity reaches record high in the U.S. – Poll'. *Newsweek*, 6 April. Available at: www.newsweek.com/vladimir-putin-popularity-us-record-high-poll-1793000 (accessed 3 October 2023).

Cox, G.W. (2009) 'Authoritarian elections and leadership succession, 1975–2004', in *APSA 2009 Toronto Meeting Paper*.

Croissant, A., Kuehn, D. and Eschenauer, T. (2018) 'Mass protests and the military', *Journal of Democracy*, 29 (3): 141–55.

Dahlum, S. (2019) 'Students in the streets: education and nonviolent protest'. *Comparative Political Studies*, 52 (2): 277–309.

Davenport, C. (2007) 'State repression and the tyrannical peace', *Journal of Peace Research*, 44 (4): 485–504.

Davenport, C. (2015) *How Social Movements Die*. Cambridge: Cambridge University Press.

Davenport, C. and Armstrong, D.A. (2004) 'Democracy and the violation of human rights: a statistical analysis from 1976 to 1996', *American Journal of Political Science*, 48 (3): 538–54.

Debs, A. (2016) 'Living by the sword and dying by the sword? Leadership transitions in and out of dictatorships', *International Studies Quarterly*, 60 (1): 73–84.

De Kadt, E. (2002) 'The military in politics: old wine in new bottles?', *Political Armies: The Military and Nation Building in the Age of Democracy*. London: Zed Books. pp. 320–1.

Diamond, L. (1999) *Developing Democracy: Toward Consolidation*. Baltimore, MD: Johns Hopkins University Press.

Diamond, L. (2002) 'Elections without democracy: thinking about hybrid regimes', *Journal of Democracy*, 13 (2): 21–35.

Dimitrov, M.K. and Sassoon, J. (2014) 'State security, information, and repression: a comparison of communist Bulgaria and Ba'thist Iraq', *Journal of Cold War Studies*, 16 (2): 3–31.

Dimitrova, A.L., Frear, M.J., Mazepus, H., Toshkov, D.D., Boroda, M., Chulitskaya, T., Grytsenko, O., Munteanu, I., Parvan, T. and Ramasheuskaya, I. (2017) 'The elements of Russia's soft power: channels, tools, and actors promoting Russian influence in the Eastern partnership countries', *EU-STRAT Working Paper Series, 2017* (4): 1–50.

Dupuy, K.E., Ron, J. and Prakash, A. (2015) 'Who survived? Ethiopia's regulatory crackdown on foreign-funded NGOs', *Review of International Political Economy*, 22 (2): 419–56.

Egorov, G., Guriev, S. and Sonin, K. (2009) 'Why resource-poor dictators allow freer media: a theory and evidence from panel data', *American Political Science Review*, 103 (4): 645–68.

Eisenstadt, T.A. (2003) *Courting Democracy in Mexico: Party Strategies and Electoral Institutions*. Cambridge: Cambridge University Press.

Eizenga, D. and Villalón, L.A. (2020) 'The undoing of a semi-authoritarian regime: the term limit debate and the fall of Blaise Compaoré in Burkina Faso', in J.R. MMangala (ed.), *The Politics of Challenging Presidential Term Limits in Africa*. Cham: Palgrave Macmillan. pp. 141–70.

El Baradei, L. (2011) 'Parallel structures in the Egyptian government bureaucracy: a problematic quick fix', *Public Administration*, 89 (4): 1351–66.

Ellyat, H. (2022) 'Nord Stream 2 cost $11 billion to build. Now, the Russia-Europe gas pipeline is unused and abandoned', CNBC, 31 March. Available at: www.cnbc.com/2022/03/31/the-nord-stream-2-pipeline-lies-abandoned-after-russia-invaded-ukraine.html (accessed 3 Oxtober 2023).

Enikolopov, R., Makarin, A. and Petrova, M. (2020) 'Social media and protest participation: evidence from Russia', *Econometrica*, 88 (4): 1479–514.

Ercan, S.A. and Gagnon, J.P. (2014) 'The crisis of democracy: Which crisis? Which democracy?', *Democratic Theory*, 1 (2): 1–10.

Esberg, J. (2020) 'All the President's trolls: Real and fake Twitter fights in El Salvador', International Crisis Group, 13 July. Available at: www.crisisgroup.org/latin-america-caribbean/central-america/el-salvador/all-presidents-trolls-real-and-fake-twitter-fights-el-salvador (accessed 10 November 2023).

Escribà-Folch, A. (2013) 'Repression, political threats, and survival under autocracy', *International Political Science Review*, 34 (5): 543–60.

Ezrow, N. (2017) 'Global politics and violent non-state actors', *Global Politics and Violent Non-state Actors*. London: Sage Publications.

Ezrow, N.M. and Frantz, E. (2011) *Dictators and Dictatorships: Understanding Authoritarian Regimes and their Leaders*. New York: Bloomsbury.

Ezrow, N.M. and Frantz, E. (2013) *Failed States and Institutional Decay: Understanding Instability and Poverty in the Developing World*. New York: Bloomsbury.

Fan, J., Zhang, T. and Zhu, Y. (2016) 'Behind the personality Cult of Xi Jinping: he may be China's most powerful leader in decades', *Foreign Policy*, I March. Available at: https://foreignpolicy.com/2016/03/08/the-personality-cult-of-xi-jinping-china-leader-communist-party/ (accessed 3. October 2023).

Feay, S. (2019) 'Undercover: inside the Chinese digital gulag, ITV – chilling insight. *Financial Times*, 12 July. Available at: www.ft.com/content/b3ecae28-a304-11e9-974c-ad1c6ab5efd1 (accessed 3 October 2023).

Fewsmith, J. and Nathan, A.J. (2019) 'Authoritarian resilience revisited: Joseph Fewsmith with response from Andrew J. Nathan', *Journal of Contemporary China*, 28 (116): 167–79.

Finkel, E., Gehlbach, S. and Olsen, T.D. (2015) 'Does reform prevent rebellion? Evidence from Russia's emancipation of the serfs', *Comparative Political Studies*, 48 (8): 984–1019.

Fish, M.S. (2017) 'The Kremlin emboldened: what is Putinism?', *Journal of Democracy*, 28 (4): 61–75.

Fish, M.S. (2018) 'What has Russia become?', *Comparative Politics*, 50 (3): 327–46.

Flintoff, C. (2012) 'Mali's coup: echoes from a turbulent past', National Public Radio, 23 March. Available at: www.npr.org/2012/03/23/149223151/malis-coup-a-setback-for-a-young-african-democracy (accessed 3 October 2023).

Francisco, R. (2004) 'After the massacre: mobilization in the wake of harsh repression', *Mobilization: An International Quarterly*, 9 (2): 107–26.

Frantz, E. and Ezrow, N. (2011) 'The politics of dictatorship', in E. Frantz and N. Ezrow, *The Politics of Dictatorship*. Boulder, CO: Lynne Rienner.

Frantz, E., Kendall-Taylor, A., Nietsche, C. and Wright, J. (2021) 'How personalist politics is changing democracies', in *Journal of Democracy*, 32 (3): 94–108.

Freyburg, T. and Garbe, L. (2018) 'Blocking the bottleneck: internet shutdowns and ownership at election times in sub-Saharan Africa', *International Journal of Communication*, 12: 3896–916.

Friedrich, C. and Brzezinski, Z. (1956) *Totalitarianism, Dictatorship and Autocracy*. Cambridge, MA: Harvard University Press.

Fröhlich, S. (2022) 'Dictators in Africa using social media to cling to power'. DW, 1 September. Available at: www.dw.com/en/dictators-in-africa-using-social-media-to-cling-to-power/a-60360543 (accessed 13 October 2023).

Gandhi, J. and Przeworski, A. (2007) 'Authoritarian institutions and the survival of autocrats', *Comparative Political Studies*, 40 (11): 1279–301.

Geddes, B. (1999) 'What do we know about democratization after twenty years?', *Annual Review of Political Science*, 2 (1): 115–44.

Geddes, B. (2003) *Paradigms and Sand Castles: Theory Building and Research Design in Comparative Politics*. Ann Arbor, MA: University of Michigan Press.

Geddes, B. (2005) September. 'Why parties and elections in authoritarian regimes?', in *Annual Meeting of the American Political Science Association*, September (pp. 456–71).

Geddes, B., Wright, J. and Frantz, E. (2014) 'Autocratic breakdown and regime transitions: a new data set', *Perspectives on Politics*, 12 (2): 313–31.

George, C. (2019) 'Journalism and authoritarian resilience', in K. Wahl-Jorgensen and T. Hamitzsch (eds), *The Handbook of Journalism Studies*. New York: Routledge. pp. 538–54.

Gerschewski, J. and Dukalskis, A. (2018) 'How the internet can reinforce authoritarian regimes: the case of North Korea', *Georgetown Journal of International Affairs*. 19: 12.

Ginkel, J. and Smith, A. (1999) 'So you say you want a revolution: a game theoretic explanation of revolution in repressive regimes', *Journal of Conflict Resolution*, 43 (3): 291–316.

Ginsburg, T. and Moustafa, T. (2008) 'Rule by law: the politics of courts in authoritarian regimes', Cambridge: Cambridge University Press.

Gleditsch, K.S. and Ward, M.D. (2006) 'Diffusion and the international context of democratization', *International Organization*, 60 (4): 911–33.

Gohdes, A.R. (2014) 'Repression in the digital age: communication technology and the politics of state violence', University of Mannheim. Ph.D. dissertation.

Gohdes, A.R. (2020) 'Repression technology: internet accessibility and state violence', *American Journal of Political Science*, 64 (3): 488–503.

Goldstone, J.A. (2001) 'Toward a fourth generation of revolutionary theory', *Annual Review of Political Science*, 4 (1): 139–87.

Green, E. (2011) 'Patronage as institutional choice: evidence from Rwanda and Uganda', *Comparative Politics*, 43 (4): 421–38.

Grewal, S. (2021) 'Why Sudan succeeded where Algeria failed', *Journal of Democracy*, 32 (4): 102–14.

Grinberg, D. (2017) 'Chilling developments: digital access, surveillance, and the authoritarian dilemma in Ethiopia', *Surveillance & Society*', 15 (3/4): 432–8.

Gueorguiev, D.D. (2018) 'Dictator's shadow: Chinese elite politics under Xi Jinping', *China Perspectives*: (2018/1–2): 17–26.

Gunitsky, S. (2015) 'Corrupting the cyber-commons: social media as a tool of autocratic stability', *Perspectives on Politics*, 13 (1): 42–54.

Guriev, S. and Treisman, D. (2019) 'Informational autocrats', *Journal of Economic Perspectives*, 33 (4): 100–27.

Guriev, S. and Treisman, D. (2020) 'A theory of informational autocracy', *Journal of Public Economics*, 186: 104–58.

Guriev, S. and Treisman, D. (2022) *Spin Dictators: The Changing Face of Tyranny in the 21st Century*. Princeton, NJ: Princeton University Press.

Hadenius, A. and Teorell, J. (2006) *Authoritarian Regimes: Stability, Change, and Pathways to Democracy, 1972–2003*. Notre Dame, IN: Helen Kellogg Institute for International Studies. pp. 1–35.

Hadenius, A. and Teorell, J. (2007) 'Pathways from authoritarianism', *Journal of Democracy*, 18 (1): 143–57.

Haggard, S. and Kaufman, R.R. (2016) 'Democratization during the third wave', *Annual Review of Political Science*, 19: 125–44.

Haggard, S. and Noland, M. (2009) 'Repression and punishment in North Korea: survey of prison camp experiences', *East–West Center Working Paper Series*, October, 20: 1–43.

Hale, H.E. (2019) 'How should we now conceptualize protest, diffusion, and regime change?', *Journal of Conflict Resolution*, 63 (10): 2402–15.

Hall, S.G. and Ambrosio, T. (2017) 'Authoritarian learning: a conceptual overview', *East European Politics*, 33 (2): 143–61.

Hall-Matthews, D. (2007) 'Tickling donors and tackling opponents: the anti-corruption campaign in Malawi', in S. Bracking (ed.), *Corruption and Development: The Anti-Corruption Campaigns*. Basingstoke: Palgrave Macmillan. pp.77–102.

Hart, B. (2021) 'Xi Jinping's cult of personality gets a big boost', *New York Magazine*, 11 November. Available at: https://nymag.com/

intelligencer/2021/11/xi-jinpings-cult-of-personality-gets-a-big-boost.html (accessed 3 October 2023).

Hashim, A. (2011) 'The Egyptian military, part two: from Mubarak onward'. *Middle East Policy*, 18 (4): 106.

Heath, J.A., Mason, T.D., Smith, W.T. and Weingarten, J.P. (2000) 'The calculus of fear: revolution, repression, and the rational peasant', *Social Science Quarterly*, pp. 622–33.

Helms, L. (2020) 'Leadership succession in politics: the democracy/autocracy divide revisited', *The British Journal of Politics and International Relations*, 22 (2): 328–46.

Hilsum, L. (2021) '"Agent of foreign interests": Museveni lashes out at Uganda election rival', *The Guardian*, 11 January. Available at: www.theguardian.com/global-development/2021/jan/11/yoweri-museveni-bobi-wine-uganda-election (accessed 3 October 2023).

Holbig, H. (2020) 'Be water, my friend: Hong Kong's 2019 anti-extradition protests', *International Journal of Sociology*, 50 (4): 325–37.

Hopkins, V. (2022) 'Ukrainians find the relatives in Russia don't believe it's a war', *New York Times*, 6 March. Available at: www.nytimes.com/2022/03/06/world/europe/ukraine-russia-families.html (accessed 3 October 2023).

Howard, M.M. and Roessler, P.G. (2006) 'Liberalizing electoral outcomes in competitive authoritarian regimes', *American Journal of Political Science*, 50 (2): 365–81.

Howells, L. and Henry, L.A. (2021) 'Varieties of digital authoritarianism: analyzing Russia's approach to Internet governance', *Communist and Post-communist Studies*, 54 (4): 1–27.

Hsieh, C.T., Miguel, E., Ortega, D. and Rodriguez, F. (2011) 'The price of political opposition: evidence from Venezuela's maisanta', *American Economic Journal: Applied Economics*, 3 (2): 196–214.

Huang, H., Boranbay-Akan, S. and Huang, L. (2019) 'Media, protest diffusion, and authoritarian resilience', *Political Science Research and Methods*, 7 (1): 23–42.

Human Rights Watch (2014) 'Jordan: terrorism amendments threaten rights'. Available at: www.hrw.org/news/2014/05/17/jordan-terrorism-amendments-threaten-rights (accessed 3 October 2023)/

Human Rights Watch (2021) *World Report*. Available at: www.hrw.org/world-report/2021/country-chapters/zimbabwe (accessed 3 October 2023).

Human Rights Watch (2022) *World Report*. Available at: www.hrw.org/world-report/2022/country-chapters/afghanistan (accessed 3 Otober 2023).

Huntington, S.P. (1993) *The Third Wave: Democratization in the Late Twentieth Century* (Vol. 4). Norman, OK: University of Oklahoma Press.

i Coma, F.M. and Morgenbesser, L. (2020) 'Election turnout in authoritarian regimes', *Electoral Studies*, 68, p. 102222.

Ifteqar, N. (2022) 'Influencers in Saudi Arabia must now obtain a permit to post ads on social media. *Vogue Middle East*, 11 August. Available at: https://en.vogue.me/culture/saudi-arabia-social-media-influencer-advertisement-permit/ (accessed 3 October 2023).

Ives, B. and Lewis, J.S. (2020) 'From rallies to riots: why some protests become violent', *Journal of Conflict Resolution*, 64 (5): 958–86.

Jarenpanit, T. (2015) 'The nonviolent political movements: case study of people alliance for democracy and people power revolution', *Political Science and Public Administration Journal*, 6 (1–2): 147–75.

Jasper, J.M. and Goodwin, J. (eds) (2011) *Contention in Context: Political Opportunities and the Emergence of Protest*. Stanford, CA: Stanford University Press.

Jayasinghe, U., Ghoshal, D. and Karunatilake, W. (2022) 'Sri Lankan president flees to Maldives, protesters storm prime minister's office', Reuters, 13 July. Available at: www.reuters.com/world/asia-pacific/sri-lanka-president-gotabaya-rajapaksa-flees-country-ap-2022-07-12/ (accessed 3 October 2023).

Jong-A-Pin, R. and Mierau, J.O. (2022) 'No country for old men: aging dictators and economic growth', *Economic Modelling*, 107, p. 105714.

Jost, J.T., Barberá, P., Bonneau, R., Langer, M., Metzger, M., Nagler, J., Sterling, J. and Tucker, J.A. (2018) 'How social media facilitates political protest: information, motivation, and social networks', *Political Psychology*, 39, pp. 85–118.

Kahn, C. and Aburto, W. (2022) 'Nicaragua has convicted more than a dozen opponents of President Daniel Ortega', National Public Radio, 11 February. Available at: www.npr.org/2022/02/11/1080204905/nicaragua-has-convicted-more-than-a-dozen-opponents-of-president-daniel-ortega (accessed 3 October 2023).

Kalathil, S. and Boas, T.C. (2003) 'Open networks, closed regimes: the impact of the Internet on authoritarian rules', Washington, DC, Carnegie Endowment for International Peace.

Kallis, A. (2002) *Fascist Ideology: Territory and Expansionism in Italy and Germany, 1922–1945*. London: Routledge.

Karaveli, H. (2014) 'Erdogan's Achilles' Heel', *Foreign Affairs*, 8 (08).

Kendall-Taylor, A. and Frantz, E. (2014) 'Mimicking democracy to prolong autocracies', *The Washington Quarterly*, 37 (4): 71–84.

Kendall-Taylor, A. and Frantz, E. (2015) 'When dictators die', *Foreign Policy*, 10 September. Available at: https://foreignpolicy.com/2015/09/10/when-dictators-die/ (accessed 3 October 2023).

Kendall-Taylor, A., Frantz, E. and Wright, J. (2017) 'The global rise of personalized politics: it's not just dictators anymore', *The Washington Quarterly*, 40 (1): 7–19.
Kendall-Taylor, A., Frantz, E. and Wright, J. (2020) 'The digital dictators: how technology strengthens autocracy', *Foreign Afairs*, 99: 103.
Kendall-Taylor, A., Lindstaedt, N. and Frantz, E. (2019) *Democracies and Authoritarian Regimes*. New York: Oxford University Press.
Kim, S. (2018) 'Candlelight for our country's right name: a Confucian interpretation of South Korea's candlelight revolution', *Religions*, 9 (11): 330.
Kim, Y.G. (2001) 'Ideological changes in North Korea since the 1990s', in *Second Biennial Conference of Korean Studies Association of Australasia,* 24 September, Monash University, Melbourne. pp. 384–92.
King, G., Pan, J. and Roberts, M.E. (2013) 'How censorship in China allows government criticism but silences collective expression', *American Political Science Review*, 107 (2): 326–43.
Kirchgaessner, S. (2021) 'Saudi Arabia jails alleged satirist "identified in Twitter infiltration"', *The Guardian*, 9 February. Available at: www.theguardian.com/world/2021/apr/09/saudi-arabia-jails-alleged-satirist-identified-in-twitter-infiltration (accessed 3 October 2023).
Kneuer, M. and Demmelhuber, T. (2016) 'Gravity centres of authoritarian rule: a conceptual approach', *Democratization*, 23 (5): 775–96.
Knutsen, C.H., Nygård, H.M. and Wig, T. (2017) 'Autocratic elections: stabilizing tool or force for change?', *World Politics*, 69 (1): 98–143.
Kuran, T. (1991) 'Now out of never: the element of surprise in the East European revolution of 1989', *World Politics*, 44 (1): 7–48.
Kurowska, X. and Reshetnikov, A. (2018a) 'Neutrollization: industrialized trolling as a pro-Kremlin strategy of desecuritization', *Security Dialogue*, 49 (5): 345–63.
Kurowska, X. and Reshetnikov, A. (2018b) 'Russia's trolling complex at home and abroad', in N. Popescu and S. Secrieru (eds), *Hacks, Leaks and Disruptions: Russian Cyber Strategies*. Paris: EU Institute for Security Studies. p. 29.
Kurtz, L.R. and Smithey, L.A. (eds) (2018) *The Paradox of Repression and Nonviolent Movements*. New York: Syracuse University Press.
The Kyiv Independent (2022) 'Forbes estimates Russia has spent $82 billion on war with Ukraine since Feb. 24', 25 November. Available at: https://kyivindependent.com/forbes-estimates-russia-has-spent-82-billion-on-war-with-ukraine-since-feb-24/ (accessed 3 October 2023).
Lachapelle, J. and Hellmeier, S. (2022) 'Pathways to democracy after authoritarian breakdown: comparative case selection and lessons from the past', *International Political Science Review*, p. 01925121221138408.

Lamensch, M. (2021) 'Authoritarianism has been reinvented for the digital age', Center for International Governance Innovation'. Available at: www. cigionline. org/articles/authoritarianism-has-been-reinvented-for-the-digital-age (accessed 3 October 2023).
Lankina, T. and Niemczyk, K. (2015) 'Russia's foreign policy and soft power', in D. Cadler (ed.), *Russia's Foreign Policy: Ideas, Domestic Politics and External Relations*. Basingstoke: Palgrave Macmillan. pp. 97–113.
Lankina, T., Libman, A. and Obydenkova, A. (2016) 'Authoritarian and democratic diffusion in post-communist regions', *Comparative Political Studies*, 49 (12): 1599–629.
Levada Centre (2023) 'Putin's approval rating'. Available at: www.levada.ru/en/ratings/ (accessed 10 November 2023).
Levitsky, S. and Way, L.A. (2002) 'Elections without democracy: the rise of competitive authoritarianism', *Journal of Democracy*, 13 (2): 51–65.
Levitsky, S. and Way, L.A. (2010) *Competitive Authoritarianism: Hybrid Regimes after the Cold War*. Cambridge: Cambridge University Press.
Lichbach, M.I. (1987) 'Deterrence or escalation? The puzzle of aggregate studies of repression and dissent', *Journal of Conflict Resolution*, 31 (2): 266–97.
Lichbach, M.I. (1998) *The Rebel's Dilemma*. Ann Arbor, MI: University of Michigan Press.
Linz, J.J. (2000) *Totalitarian and Authoritarian Regimes*. Boulder, CO: Lynne Rienner.
Lonkila, M., Shpakovskaya, L. and Torchinsky, P. (2021) 'Digital activism in Russia: the evolution and forms of online participation in an authoritarian state', in D. Gritsenko, M. Wijermars and M. Kopotev (eds), *The Palgrave Handbook of Digital Russia Studies*. Basingstoke: Palgrave Macmillan. pp.135–53.
Louis, A. (2021) 'Human rights violations in Belarus require an international Investigation', Council of Europe, June, pp. 1–17. Available at: https://assembly.coe.int/LifeRay/JUR/Pdf/TextesProvisoires/2021/20210324-BelarusViolationsHR-EN.pdf (accessed 3 October 2023).
Lu, J. and Zhao, Y. (2018) 'Implicit and explicit control: modeling the effect of internet censorship on political protest in China', *International Journal of Communication*, 12: 23.
Lührmann, A. and Lindberg, S.I. (2019) 'A third wave of autocratization is here: what is new about it?' *Democratization*, 26 (7): 1095–113.
Luqiu, L.R. (2016) 'The reappearance of the cult of personality in China', *East Asia*, 33 (4): 289–307.
Lust-Okar, E. (2005) *Structuring Conflict in the Arab World: Incumbents, Opponents, and Institutions*. Cambridge: Cambridge University Press.

Lust-Okar, E. (2006) 'Elections under authoritarianism: preliminary lessons from Jordan', *Democratization*, 13 (3): 456–71.

Lust-Okar, E. (2009) 'Reinforcing informal institutions through authoritarian elections: insights from Jordan', *Middle East Law and Governance*, 1 (1): 3–37.

MacKinnon, R. (2009) 'China's censorship 2.0: How companies censor bloggers', *First Monday*, 14 (2).

MacKinnon, R., Hickok, E., Bar, A. and Lim, H.I. (2015) *Fostering Freedom Online: The Role of Internet Intermediaries*. Paris: UNESCO Publishing.

Maeda, K. (2010) 'Two modes of democratic breakdown: a competing risks analysis of democratic durability', *The Journal of Politics*, 72 (4): 1129–143.

Magaloni, B. (2006) *Voting for Autocracy: Hegemonic Party Survival and its Demise in Mexico* (Vol. 296). Cambridge: Cambridge University Press. p. 30.

Magaloni, B. (2008) 'Credible power-sharing and the longevity of authoritarian rule', *Comparative Political Studies*, 41 (4–5): 715–41.

Magaloni, B. and Kricheli, R. (2010) 'Political order and one-party rule', *Annual Review of Political Science*, 13: 12343.

Malesky, E. and Schuler, P. (2011) 'The single-party dictator's dilemma: information in elections without opposition', *Legislative Studies Quarterly*, 36 (4): 491–530.

Mare, A. (2020) 'Internet shutdowns in Africa, state-ordered internet shutdowns and digital authoritarianism in Zimbabwe', *International Journal of Communication*, 14: 20.

Martinez-Bravo, M., i Miquel, G.P., Qian, N. and Yao, Y. (2014) *Political Reform in China: The Effect of Local Elections*. NBER Working Paper, 18101. Cambridge, MA: National Bureau of Economic Research.

Mayr, W. (2009) 'Romania's bloody revolution: 20 years later'. *ABC News*, 21 October. Available at: https://abcnews.go.com/WN/romanias-bloody-revolution-20-years/story?id=8877685_(accessed 3 October 2023).

Mechkova, V., Pemstein, D., Seim, B. and Wilson, S. (2022) *Measuring Internet Politics: Digital Society Project (DSP), Annual Report v4.*

Melly, P. (2021) 'Mali coup: how to solve the conundrum', BBC News, 27 May. Available at: www.bbc.co.uk/news/world-africa-57255601 (accessed 3 October 2023).

Meredith, K. (2013) 'Social media and cyber utopianism: civil society versus the Russian state during the "White Revolution" 2011–2012', *St Antony's International Review*, 8 (2): 89–105.

Michaelsen, M. (2018) 'Exit and voice in a digital age: Iran's exiled activists and the authoritarian state', *Globalizations*, 15 (2): 248–64.

Moore, W.H. (2000) 'The repression of dissent: a substitution model of government coercion', *Journal of Conflict Resolution*, 44 (1): 107–27.

Morgan, P. (2003) *Fascism in Europe, 1919–1945*. Abingdon: Routledge.

Morgenbesser, L. (2019) 'Cambodia's transition to hegemonic authoritarianism', *Journal of Democracy*, 30 (1): 158–71.

Morgus, R. (2019) 'The spread of Russia's digital authoritarianism', in N.D. Wright (ed.), *Artificial Intelligence, China, Russia, and the Global Order/ed.* Maxwell Air Force Base, Alabama: Air University Press.

Moustafa, T. (2007) *The Struggle for Constitutional Power: Law, Politics, and Economic Development in Egypt*. Cambridge: Cambridge University Press.

Mueller, L. (2020) 'What is African about African protests?', *SAIS Review of International Affairs*, 40 (2): 65–75.

Oh, K. and Hassig, R. (2000) *North Korea: through the looking glass*. Washington. DC: Brookings Institution.

Olar, R.G. (2019) 'Do they know something we don't? Diffusion of repression in authoritarian regimes'. *Journal of Peace Research*, 56 (5), 667–81.

Osa, M. and Schock, K. (2007) 'A long, hard slog: political opportunities, social networks and the mobilization of dissent in non-democracies', in *Research in Social Movements, Conflicts and Change* (Vol. 27). Leeds: Emerald. pp. 123–53.

Panov, P. and Ross, C. (2013) 'Patterns of electoral contestation in Russian regional assemblies: between "competitive" and "hegemonic" authoritarianism', *Demokratizatsiya*, 21 (3): 369.

Patel, D.S. (2015) 'The more things change, the more they stay the same: Jordanian Islamist responses in spring and fall', *Project on United States Relations with the Islamic World*, Working Paper. Washington, DC: Brookings Institution.

Patel, D., Bunce, V. and Wolchik, S. (2014) '3. Diffusion and demonstration', in M. Lynch (ed.), *The Arab Uprisings Explained*. New York City: Columbia University Press. pp. 57–74.

Pelke, L. and Croissant, A. (2021) 'Conceptualizing and measuring autocratization episodes', *Swiss Political Science Review*, 27 (2): 434–48.

Pierskalla, J.H. (2010) 'Protest, deterrence, and escalation: the strategic calculus of government repression', *Journal of Conflict Resolution*, 54 (1): 117–45.

Ploch, L. (2008) 'Zimbabwe: 2008 elections and implications for US policy', September, Library of Congress. Washington, DC: Congressional Research Service.

Polyakova, A. and Meserole, C. (2019) *Exporting Digital Authoritarianism: The Russian and Chinese Models*, in Policy Brief, Democracy and Disorder Series. *Foreign Policy*. Washington, DC: Brookings. pp.1–22.

Powell, J. and Thyne, D. (2011) 'Global instances of coups from 1950-present', *Journal of Peace Research*, 48 (2): 249–59.

Powell, J. and Thyne, D. (2022) https://arresteddictatorship.com/coups/

Przeworski, A. (1991) *Democracy and the Market: Political and Economic Reforms in Eastern Europe and Latin America*. Cambridge: Cambridge University Press.

Qiang, X. (2019) 'The road to digital unfreedom: President Xi's surveillance state', *Journal of Democracy*, 30 (1): 53–67.

Qiang, X. (2021) 'Chinese digital authoritarianism and its global impact', in M. Lynch, *Digital Activism and Authoritarian Adaptation in the Middle East*, p. 35.

Qin, B., Strömberg, D. and Wu, Y. (2017) 'Why does China allow freer social media? Protests versus surveillance and propaganda', *Journal of Economic Perspectives*, 31 (1): 117–40.

Regan, P.M. and Henderson, E.A. (2002) 'Democracy, threats and political repression in developing countries: are democracies internally less violent?', *Third World Quarterly*, 23 (1): 119–36.

Reuter, O.J. and Robertson, G.B. (2015) 'Legislatures, co-optation, and social protest in contemporary authoritarian regimes', *The Journal of Politics*, 77 (1): 235–48.

Reuters (2008) 'Turkmenistan ends ban on opera and circus', 21 January. Available at: www.reuters.com/article/uk-turkmenistan-opera-idUKL2129776520080121 (accessed 3 October 2023).

Roberts, M.E. (2018) *Censored: Distraction and Diversion Inside China's Great Firewall*. Princeton, NJ: Princeton University Press.

Roberts, S. and Ziemer, U. (2018) 'Explaining the pattern of Russian authoritarian diffusion in Armenia', *East European Politics*, 34 (2): 152–72.

Rød, E.G. and Weidmann, N.B. (2015) 'Empowering activists or autocrats? The Internet in authoritarian regimes', *Journal of Peace Research*, 52 (3): 338–51.

Roth, A. (2018) 'Russia blocks millions of IP addresses in battle against Telegram app', *The Guardian*, 17 April. Available at: www.theguardian.com/world/2018/apr/17/russia-blocks-millions-of-ip-addresses-in-battle-against-telegram-app (accessed 3 October 2023).

Roucek, J.S. (1962) 'Yemen in geopolitics', *Contemporary Review*, 202 (1163): 310–17.

Ruijgrok, K. (2017) 'From the web to the streets: internet and protests under authoritarian regimes', *Democratization*, 24 (3): 498–520.

Ruwitch, J. (2023) 'China's Xi Jinping, as expected, gets 5 more years as state president'. National Public Radio, 10 March. Available at: www.npr.org/2023/03/10/1162128750/chinas-xi-jinping-5-more-years-as-president (accessed 3 October 2023).

Safaei, S. (2023) 'Iran's protests are nowhere near revolutionary', *Foreign Policy*, 17 January. Available at: https://foreignpolicy.com/2023/01/17/irans-protests-are-nowhere-near-revolutionary/ (accessed 3 October 2023).

Samset, I. (2011) 'Building a repressive peace: The case of post-genocide Rwanda', *Journal of Intervention and Statebuilding*, 5 (3): 265–83.

Sanches, E.R. (2022) 'Introduction: Zooming in on protest and change in Africa', in *Popular Protest, Political Opportunities, and Change in Africa*. Abingdon: Routledge. pp.1–18.

Schedler, A. (2002) 'The menu of manipulation', *Journal of Democracy*, 13: 36.

Schedler, A. (2010) 'Democracy's past and future: authoritarianism's last line of defense', *Journal of Democracy*, 21 (1): 69–80.

Schmitz, R. (2021) 'As Hungary cuts radio station, critics say Europe should put Orban on notice'. National Public Radio, 8 March. Available at: www.npr.org/2021/03/08/974202772/as-hungary-cuts-radio-station-critics-say-europe-should-put-orban-on-notice (accessed 3 October 2023).

Schraeder, P.J. and Redissi, H. (2011) 'The upheavals in Egypt and Tunisia: Ben Ali's fall', *Journal of Democracy*, 22 (3): 5–19.

Scurtu, I. (2010) 'The Romanian revolution of December 1989', *Annals of the Academy of Romanian Scientists Series on History and Archaelogy*, 2 (2): 60–109.

Serino, K. (2023) 'Here's what's different about the Brazil attack compared to Jan. 6', PBS 13 January. Available at: www.pbs.org/newshour/world/what-the-attack-in-brazil-says-about-far-right-movements-around-the-world (accessed 3 October 2023).

Shahbaz, A. (2018) 'The rise of digital authoritarianism: Freedom on the net 2018', *Freedom House*. Available at: https://freedomhouse.org/report/freedom-net/2018/rise-digital-authoritarianism

Shahbaz, A. and Funk, A. (2019) 'Freedom on the net 2019: the crisis of social media', *Freedom House*, 4: 2019–11.

Shambaugh, D. (2015) 'China's soft-power push: the search for respect', *Foreign Affairs*, 94 (4): 99–107.

Shirk, S.L. (2018) 'China in Xi's' new era: the return to personalistic rule', *Journal of Democracy*, 29 (2): 22–36.

Sinkkonen, E. and Lassila, J. (2022) 'Digital authoritarianism and technological cooperation in Sino-Russian relations: common goals and diverging standpoints', in S. Kirchberger, S. Sinjen and N. Wörmer (eds), *Russia–China Relations: Emerging Alliance or Eternal Rivals?* Cham: Springer. pp. 165–84.

Slater, D. and Wong, J. (2013) 'The strength to concede: ruling parties and democratization in developmental Asia', *Perspectives on Politics*, 11 (3): 717–33.

Smith, B. (2005) 'Life of the party: the origins of regime breakdown and persistence under single-party rule', *World Politics*, 57 (3): 421–51.

Smyth, R. and Turovsky, R. (2018) 'Legitimising victories: electoral authoritarian control in Russia's gubernatorial elections', *Europe–Asia Studies*, 70 (2): 182–201.

Snyder. T. (2010) *Bloodlands: Europe between Hitler and Stalin.* New York: Basic Books.

Soldatov, A. and Borogan, I. (2017) *The Red Web: The Kremlin's Wars on the Internet*. New York: Perseus Books.

Solomon, P.H. (2007) 'Courts and judges in authoritarian regimes', *World Politics*, 60 (1): 122–45.

Stewart, P. and Ali, I. (2022) 'More than 100,000 Russian military casualties in Ukraine, top U.S. general says', Reuters, 10 November. Available at: www.reuters.com/world/europe/more-than-100000-russian-military-casualties-ukraine-top-us-general-2022-11-10/ (accessed 3 October 2023).

Strangio, S. (2022) 'Cambodia readies third mass trial of opposition officials', *The Diplomat*, 24 August. Available at: https://thediplomat.com/2022/08/cambodia-readies-third-mass-trial-of-opposition-officials/ (accessed 3 October 2023).

Stockmann, D. and Gallagher, M.E. (2011) 'Remote control: how the media sustain authoritarian rule in China', *Comparative Political Studies*, 44 (4): 436–67.

Sullivan, C.M. (2016) 'Undermining resistance: mobilization, repression, and the enforcement of political order', *Journal of Conflict Resolution*, 60 (7): 1163–90.

Sutton, J., Butcher, C.R. and Svensson, I. (2014) 'Explaining political jiu-jitsu: institution-building and the outcomes of regime violence against unarmed protests', *Journal of Peace Research*, 51 (5): 559–73.

Tanaka, S. (2018) 'Aging gracefully? Why old autocrats hold competitive elections', *Asian Journal of Comparative Politics*, 3 (1): 81–102.

Tarrow, S. (1998) 'The very excess of democracy: state building and contentious politics in America', in A.N. Costain and A.S. McFarland (eds), *Social Movements and American Political institutions*. Washington, DC: Rowman & Littlefield. pp. 20–38.

Taylor, L. (2021) 'The myth of "stray bullets" in Uganda', *Foreign Policy*, 18 November. Available at: https://foreignpolicy.com/2021/11/18/uganda-state-violence-killings-museveni-police-protests/ (accessed 3 October 2023).

Thyen, K. and Gerschewski, J. (2018) 'Legitimacy and protest under authoritarianism: explaining student mobilization in Egypt and Morocco during the Arab uprisings', *Democratization*, 25 (1): 38–57.

Tilly, C. (2003) *The Politics of Collective Violence*. Cambridge: Cambridge University Press.

Tucker, J.A., Theocharis, Y., Roberts, M.E. and Barberá, P. (2017) 'From liberation to turmoil: social media and democracy', *Journal of Democracy*, 28 (4): 46–59.

Tudoroiu, T. (2014) 'Social media and revolutionary waves: the case of the Arab spring', *New Political Science*, 36 (3): 346–65.

Ulfelder, J. (2005) 'Contentious collective action and the breakdown of authoritarian regimes', *International Political Science Review*, 26 (3): 311–34.

United Nations Human Rights (OHCHR) (2023).'Belarus must end systematic repression, release detainees, UN Human Rights Chief says'. OHCHR, 17 March. Available at: www.ohchr.org/en/press-releases/2023/03/belarus-must-end-systematic-repression-release-detainees-un-human-rights (accessed 13 October 2023).

Van Stekelenburg, J. and Klandermans, B. (2013) 'The social psychology of protest', *Current Sociology*, 61 (5–6): 886–905.

Varieties of Democracy (2020) *Autocratization Surges – Resistance Grows: Democracy Report*, pp. 1–40. Available at: https://v-dem.net/ (accessed 3 October 2023).

Varieties of Democracy (2022) *Democracy Report*, pp. 1–60. Available at: https://v-dem.net/ (accessed 3 October 2023).

Varol, O.O. (2014) 'Stealth authoritarianism', *Iowa Law Review*, *100*, p. 1673.

Volkov, D. and Kolesnikov, A. (2022) 'My country, right or wrong: Russian public opinion on Ukraine'. Carnegie Endowment for International Peace, 7 September. Available at: https://carnegieendowment.org/2022/09/07/my-country-right-or-wrong-russian-public-opinion-on-ukraine-pub-87803 (accessed 3 October 2023).

Von Soest, C. (2015) 'Democracy prevention: the international collaboration of authoritarian regimes', *European Journal of Political Research*, 54 (4): 623–38.

Waisbord, S. and Amado, A. (2017) 'Populist communication by digital means: presidential Twitter in Latin America', *Information, Communication & Society*, 20 (9): 1330–46.

Walker, C. (2016) 'The authoritarian threat: the hijacking of "Soft Power"'. *Journal of Democracy*, 27 (1): 49–63.

Walker, C. (2018) 'What is "Sharp Power"?', *Journal of Democracy*, 29 (3): 9–23.

Wallach, A. (1991) 'Censorship in the Soviet bloc', *Art Journal*, 50 (3): 75–83.

Watts, L.L. (2019) 'The Romanian army in the December revolution and beyond', in D.N. Nelson (ed.) *Romania After Tyranny*. Abingdon: Routledge. pp. 96–126.

Weyland, K. (2012) 'The Arab Spring: why the surprising similarities with the revolutionary wave of 1848?', *Perspectives on Politics*, 10 (4): 917–34.

Wijayanto, B.S., Martini, R. and Elsitra, G.N. (2022) 'Digital authoritarianism in Southeast Asia: a systematic literature review', in *ICISPE 2021: Proceedings of the 6th International Conference on Social and Political Enquiries,* 14–15 September, Semarang, Indonesia (p. 465). European Alliance for Innovation.

Wright, J. and Escribà-Folch, A. (2012) 'Authoritarian institutions and regime survival: transitions to democracy and subsequent autocracy', *British Journal of Political Science*, 42 (2): 283–309.

Xu, X. (2021) 'To repress or to co-opt? Authoritarian control in the age of digital surveillance'. *American Journal of Political Science*, 65 (2): 309–25.

Yin, L. and Flew, T. (2018) 'Xi Dada loves Peng Mama: digital culture and the return of charismatic authority in China', *Thesis Eleven*, 144 (1): 80–99.

Yom, S.L. and Gause III, F.G. (2012) 'Resilient royals: how Arab monarchies hang on', *Journal of Democracy*, 23 (4): 74–88.

Yu, V. (2022) 'Who is Li Qiang, the man poised to become China's next premier?', *The Guardian*, 24 October. Available at: www.theguardian.com/world/2022/oct/24/who-is-li-qiang-the-man-poised-to-become-chinas-next-premier (accessed 3 October 2023).

Zaverucha, J. and da Cunha Rezende, F. (2009) How the military competes for expenditure in Brazilian democracy: arguments for an outlier'. *International Political Science Review*, 30 (4): 407–29.

Zeng, J. (2020) 'Artificial intelligence and China's authoritarian governance', *International Affairs*, 96 (6): 144–59.

Zhao, D. (2010) 'Authoritarian state and contentious politics', in K.T. Leicht and J.C. Jenkins (eds), *Handbook of Politics: State and Society in Global Perspective*.Cham: Springer. pp. 459–76.

Ziegler, C.E. (2016) 'Great powers, civil society and authoritarian diffusion in Central Asia', *Central Asian Survey*, 35 (4): 549–69.

Zisser, E. (2001) 'The Syrian army: between the domestic and the external fronts', *Middle East Review of International Affairs*, 5 (1): 1–12.

index